MOTOR C

CW01045255

A HISTC
THE EARLY M

By

JOHN H. WYATT

First published in 1925

Read & Co.

Copyright © 2021 Read & Co. Books

This edition is published by Read & Co. Books,
an imprint of Read & Co.

This book is copyright and may not be reproduced or copied in any
way without the express permission of the publisher in writing.

British Library Cataloguing-in-Publication Data
A catalogue record for this book is available
from the British Library.

Read & Co. is part of Read Books Ltd.
For more information visit
www.readandcobooks.co.uk

CONTENTS

ILLUSTRATIONS

MOTORCYCLING

Motorcycling can be a hobby, a sport, a mode of transport or a fashion statement – though for most people in the world, motorcycling is the only affordable form of individual motorized transportation.

Statistically, there is a large difference between the car-dominated developed world, and the more populous developing world, where cars are less common than motorcycles. In the developed world, motorcycles are frequently owned in addition to a car, and thus used primarily for recreation or when traffic density means a motorcycle confers travel time or parking advantages as a mode of transport. In the developing world a motorcycle is more likely to be the primary mode of transport for its owner, and often the owner's family as well. It is not uncommon for riders to transport multiple passengers or large goods aboard small motorcycles and scooters – simply because there is no better alternative.

The simplicity demanded of motorcycles, coupled with the high volume of sales possible makes them a profitable and appealing product for major manufacturers – who go to substantial lengths to attract and retain market share. Of all the motorcycles in the world, 58% are in the Asia Pacific and Southern and Eastern Asia regions, excluding car-centric Japan. In the developed world, motorcycling goes beyond being just a mode of motor transportation or sport. It is also leisure activity and numerous subcultures and lifestyles have evolved around the use of motorcycles. Although mainly a solo activity, motorcycling can be very social and motorcyclists tend to have a strong sense of community.

There are many reasons for riding a motorcycle, for most

riders, a motorcycle is a cheaper and more convenient form of transportation which causes less commuter congestion within cities and has less environmental impacts than automobile ownership. Others ride as a way to relieve stress and to 'clear their minds' as described in Robert M. Pirsig's book *Zen and the Art of Motorcycle Maintenance*. Pirsig contrasted the sense of connection experienced by motorcyclists with the isolation of drivers who are 'always in a compartment', passively observing the passing landscape. The connection to ones motorcycle is sensed further, as Pirsig explained, by the frequent need to maintain its mechanical operation.

Speed is another large factor which draws many people to motorcycling, because the power-to-weight ratios of even low-power motorcycles rivals that of an expensive sports car. The power-to-weight ratio of many modestly priced sport bikes is well beyond any mass-produced car. Hunter S. Thompson's book *Hell's Angels* includes an ode to the joys of pushing a motorcycle to its limits, 'with the throttle screwed on there is only the barest margin, and no room at all for mistakes ... that's when the strange music starts ... fear becomes exhilaration [and the] only sounds are the wind and a dull roar floating back from the mufflers' and T. E. Lawrence wrote of the 'lustfulness of moving swiftly' and the 'pleasure of speeding on the road.' A sensation he compared to feeling 'the earth moulding herself under me ... coming alive ... and heaving and tossing on each side like a sea.'

About 200 million motorcycles, including mopeds, motor scooters, motorised bicycles, and other powered two and three-wheelers, are in use worldwide, or about 33 motorcycles per 1000 people. By comparison, there are about 1 billion cars in the world, or about 141 per 1000 people, with about one third in service in Japan and the United States. Despite their popularity, motorcycles do pose significant risks however. The relative risk of a motorcycle rider being killed or seriously injured per kilometre travelled was around 54 times higher in Great Britain in 2006 than for car drivers. United States Department of Transportation data for 2005 showed that for passenger cars, 18.62 fatal crashes occur per 100,000 vehicles. For motorcycles this figure is 75.19 per 100,000 vehicles – four times higher than for cars.

To address motorcycle safety issues, motorcycle-specific training and personal protective equipment is important for motorcyclists' survival on the road, and mandated in many countries and several U.S. states and counties. Helmet usage reduces the chance for death in an accident by 40% and the risk of serious injury by 70%. While helmet usage generally is increasing world-wide and 77% of the worlds population is covered by extensive helmet laws, many countries still lack sufficient enforcement. Pakistan has both laws requiring driver and passenger to wear a helmet and regulations on helmet standards – but still, only 10% of all riders in Pakistan wear a helmet.

Motorcycling lifestyles have been adopted by many different groups spanning nations and cultures. They include commuters, mainstream motorcycle clubs such as long-distance riding clubs, adventurer touring, trail riding and those involved with motorcycle sports, such as motocross riding, drag racing, circuit racing and trick or stunt enthusiasts.

Around the world, motorcycles have historically been associated with highly visible subcultures (such as the scooter riders and cafe racer riders of the 1950s and 60s in Great Britain), and they often are seen as inhabiting the fringes of society. Numerous books about motorcycle subcultures have been written, including Hunter S. Thompson's (previously mentioned) *Hells Angels*, Lee Gutkind's *Bike Fever*, and Daniel R. Wolf's *The Rebels*. There are also several 'outlaw motorcycle gangs', occasionally getting in trouble with the law, such as the Pagans, Hells Angels, Outlaws MC, and Bandidos – known as the 'Big Four'.

Motorcycling is a truly fascinating means of transport, with fans and adherents spread out all over the globe. It is hoped that the reader enjoys this book on the subject, and is maybe inspired to try some motorcycling for themselves.

MOTOR CYCLING

A HISTORY OF THE EARLY MOTORCYCLE

The Scott Super-Squirrel Two-Speed

CHAPTER I

HISTORICAL AND INTRODUCTORY

THE history of the motor cycle does not go back far. At the beginning of the present century these machines were very scarce, and needless to say very crude.

Even in the early days, however, the pioneers had ideas of the wonderful possibilities of mechanically propelled bicycles; they were then considered extravagant, but have since been realized in part. For instance, an old print shows a man on a motor cycle flying across a river; at the present time long jumping on motor bicycles is a recognized feature of gymkhanas, and by the use of a suitable platform a distance of about sixty feet has been cleared, the machine and rider rising to a height of five or six feet at mid-distance. This sort of jumping is, of course, in a sense artificial, but a machine will often leave the ground for a few feet when crossing a hump-backed bridge at speed. A beginner is not advised to try these stunts because the machine will sometimes wobble sharply when it meets the ground again, and if not in skilful hands this may lead to disaster.

The application of power to a bicycle or tricycle was made possible by the invention of the internal combustion engine, which, as its name implies, burns its fuel inside the cyclinder and not, as in the case of a steam engine, outside a separate boiler for the generation of steam. The pressure on the piston is provided by the exploded gas, and the engine depends for its power to a large extent upon the speed at which it rotates. Naturally an engine must be small in size and light in weight if it is to be suitable for propelling a cycle; for this reason a steam engine, with its separate boiler and a burner with which to heat it, has never been successful commercially as a power unit for a bicycle, though the mechanical difficulties of fitting it can be overcome.

How an internal combustion engine works will be explained later. It is sufficient to state here that it combines considerable power with relatively light weight, and uses a fuel which can be conveniently carried in sufficient quantity for a run of nearly two hundred miles.

The motor cycle followed naturally upon the invention of the motor-car, and some very quaint motor tricycles, with the engines attached to the rear axle, were among the earliest examples. These were extraordinarily noisy and could be heard approaching when miles away, the noise getting louder and louder till they passed with a rattle and a roar only equalled by a traction engine.

At first a motor cycle was not designed throughout by an engineer; it was merely a bicycle of rather stouter build than usual with an engine attached—one might almost say stuck on, for it was fixed in any position that seemed convenient, rather than as a part of a complete and symmetrical whole. The Minerva engine was clipped low down on the tube from the head to the bottom bracket, where the pedals were situated, and drove the rear wheel through a twisted leather belt. The Wernher was attached high up in front and drove the front wheel by means of a friction wheel on the tyre. The Singer had its engine placed within the wheel, mounted on a fixed axle and driving through gears; sometimes the front wheel was equipped in this way and sometimes the rear, and wide aluminium spokes were used instead of the usual wire spokes. Oil the later models the wheel had spokes at one side only, and the engine drove forward to the countershaft and then back to the rear hub on the other side of the wheel.

These few examples show the different positions tried for the engine before it began to be built into the frame in a central position and rigidly attached as it is to-day, and would have been from the first if the problem had been approached more scientifically and motor cycles designed instead of evolved.

At first no one dreamt of supplying a motor cycle without pedalling gear, and no attempt was made to provide more than one gear ratio between the engine and the road wheel; moreover, the engines used were small and low-powered, consequently failure on hills was common and l.p.a. (which, being interpreted, meant light pedalling assistance), was commoner still. The older quadricycles, which carried two passengers and were commonly known as 'quads,' were also fitted with, engines developing no more than two and a half horse-power. Nowadays an engine rated at 2 1/2 h.p. will give an actual horsepower of perhaps four times as much, and a change-speed gear will enable the power to be maintained; but then it was not so, and when the speed fell away on a hill the available power decreased very rapidly just when it was most wanted, and the machine stopped.

Early in the present century engines began to be built into the frames instead of being clipped on. Generally engine plates and cradles were used, which were brazed into the frame, and to these the engines were bolted, the crank-case forming part of the frame. In the Bradbury motor cycles this principle was carried farther, for the frame tubes were built into the engine and met at the main-shaft axle. This gave a sound and rigid construction, but it was inconvenient when an engine needed to be taken out of the frame. On the early Humber machines the engine was enclosed in four light tubes running down the sides of the cylinder, through the sides of the crank case, and meeting in lugs above and below. This then took the place of the down tube from the bottom of the head to the crank bracket; it provided a rigid fixing, could be taken out without much difficulty, and survives to-day in the P. & M. machine, being the invention of Mr Phelon of that company (Phelon & Moore).

About this time change-speed gears began to be used, but only by a few firms. The first machine owned by the writer had two speeds. This was accomplished by having a chain on either side of the rear wheel from the countershaft to the hub. Either of these could be engaged by a dog-clutch mechanism in the hub, and thus two ratios could be obtained as required. A primary chain from the engine drove the countershaft, and the change was made by twisting the right handle grip. The thing was crude, and there was no friction clutch to take up the drive, but it worked quite well. This machine had no pedalling gear, and in many other ways it was before its time. The engine was governed on the exhaust as well as through the throttle, a method of control that was superseded by a somewhat similar governor on the inlet valve, but both have now disappeared. This was a Raleigh, and early in the present century it held the record between the Land's End and John o' Groats, driven by G. P. Mills (now Lt.-Col.).

CHAPTER II

THE CHOICE OF A MOUNT

WHILE motor cyclists are agreed on many points concerning the choice of a machine for a novice, on others the question is a very debatable one. Obviously the choice must depend very largely upon the uses to which the machine will be put; the age, sex, and strength of the rider will each have its influence, and the funds at the purchaser's disposal must also be taken into consideration.

Only in exceptional cases will it be advisable for a novice's first motor cycle to be very fast, though it is natural for a young man to desire a fast mount. A boy, girl, or elderly person, or indeed anyone not possessed of much strength, will be best suited by a light-weight machine of low, or quite moderate, power, because it will be so much easier to handle at home; it can, too, be managed more confidently on the road, for the knowledge that one has a heavy and powerful engine to look after may in itself induce a certain nervousness, especially in a rider of small physique.

It is well that every one who attempts to ride a motor cycle should have first become accustomed to the balance and steering of a two wheeler by bicycle riding. This will also have the advantage of instilling some of that desirable quality called 'road sense,' which enables one to realize quickly whether there will be plenty of time to cross in front of another vehicle, or if it will be better to decrease speed and pass behind it. The art of balancing having been previously acquired, it will be easy to pick up the driving very quickly to a sufficient extent to feel quite comfortable and at home on a motor cycle. Some soon become good drivers; others never do, because they have not the necessary feeling for things mechanical, nor the unconscious sympathy for inanimate objects, which prevents them from overdriving a suffering engine.

When the novice has made up his mind what type of machine will best suit his purpose, the next question for him to decide is whether he will buy a new machine or be content at first with a second-hand mount. There is much to be said on either side; but briefly it comes to this: a new machine will give less trouble, and in the event of a small derangement the works, or agent who supplied the machine, will put things right; a second-hand machine will more quickly give the rider an insight into roadside repairs and adjustment, for it is by encountering troubles that we learn to rectify them and thus become more self-reliant.

There is, too, another aspect of the case. It is a pity that a new and nicely finished machine should be knocked about by an inexperienced rider who might just as well serve his novitiate upon a motor cycle that has already seen service. Where money is fairly plentiful, I should advise the purchase of a second-hand mount at first. After this has been ridden for a few months and the rider has gained confidence and experience, it can be sold and a new machine purchased. A lady, however, or a man who is quite unmechanical, would do well to purchase a new machine from the start. If money be no object, then I should say that it would be better to purchase new machines and renew them at least every year. But the impecunious rider must be content with what he can afford, remembering that in the case of motor cycles—like everything else—the best is cheapest in the end, and this applies more to motor cycles than to most things.

A man who has some experience, or an experienced friend to help him, will get the best value by buying a second-hand machine privately. If he lack these advantages, it is better to go to a good dealer and rely to some extent upon his judgment. A look through the advertisement columns of the motor cycling papers will give a general idea of the prices asked for machines of different makes and ages.

On the whole, a single-cylinder engine is a wise first choice because it is more easily kept in tune than a twin- or four-cylinder, for the simple reason that it has fewer parts. Also when trouble occurs one does not have to locate the faulty cylinder as a preliminary operation. Twins are, however, just as reliable as singles, and just as easy to drive. It is a mistake to suppose, as many do, that because a twin has more parts it is more likely to go wrong, for if it be properly designed, every part will be up to its work, and, moreover, the stresses upon the gear-box and transmission will be less because the impulses from the engine are lighter and more numerous.

When tuning a single cylinder one naturally gets the compression as good as possible, but when tuning a twin it is desirable to get the compression equal in the two cylinders. Again the induction system must be more carefully watched on multi-cylinder engines. On a single, a slight air leak in the inlet pipe can be neutralized by cutting off some air at the carburetter; though this is not a good plan it will suffice at the moment, but on a twin this procedure will result in making the mixture in one cylinder too rich and the remedy will be worse than the disease.

These points will be touched upon in more detail in another chapter. My object at the moment is merely to show how differences in design should affect the choice of a machine, and that the purchaser of a twin must expect to spend a little more time upon it, if he wishes to get the best results, as nearly all motor cyclists do.

CHAPTER III

THE PRIME MOVER

IT has already been stated that a motor cycle is driven by an internal combustion engine, and at present there are two types of this engine employed. The first was known as the Otto engine, but is now always called a four-stroke, because it has four strokes in its cycle of operations; the second works on a two-stroke cycle, and is shortly called a two-stroke. Occasionally people speak of a four-cycle engine, but this is incorrect, though it might be called a four-stroke-cycle engine. A stroke is the passage of the piston from end to end of the cylinder in either direction, and therefore there are two strokes to every revolution.

In every kind of internal combustion engine now used in motor cycle practice the explosive mixture, consisting of the vapour of petrol, or some other fuel, mixed with air, is (1) taken into the cylinder, (2) compressed to make it more powerful, (3) exploded to drive the engine, and (4) driven out through the exhaust pipe and silencer when no longer any use. In the four-stroke engine each of these operations corresponds roughly to a stroke of the piston; but they do not begin and finish when the piston is at the top or bottom dead-centre, that is to say, at its highest or lowest point, the crank being at those moments directly in line with the connecting rod. The reason for this will appear later.

The Four-stroke Engine.—A four-stroke engine, then, operates as follows: while the piston is descending, *i.e.*, travelling toward the crank-axle, it draws a charge of explosive mixture into the cylinder, by what is commonly called suction, through the

21

inlet valve. This is called the induction stroke. Next comes the compression stroke, during which the mixture is compressed by the rising piston in the combustion chamber or cylinder head. The charge is then ignited by a spark from the sparking plug, and it explodes or burns very rapidly, driving the piston downward, and in this manner producing the power to drive the engine. This is known as the explosion, firing, or power stroke. Last comes the exhaust stroke, during which the rising piston drives out the burnt gases. This is the whole cycle of a four-stroke engine, and it is repeated a thousand or so times every minute. A thousand cycles per minute represents two revolutions in the same time (2000 r.p.m.); this is quite a moderate speed for a modern motor cycle engine. It will be seen that the piston acts to some extent as a pump in drawing the mixture into the engine and expelling it when used.

The inlet valve opens not on the top dead-centre, as might be expected, but a little beyond it (from 5 to 10 degrees measured in the revolution of the fly-wheel). If it opened earlier some of the exhaust gas that had not escaped would be blown into the induction pipe and retard the ingress of the fresh gas. Also it does not close exactly at the bottom of the stroke because the inertia, or impetus, of the gas in the pipe causes it to continue rushing into the cylinder after the suction has ceased. The inlet valve therefore closes about 20 degrees beyond the bottom dead-centre. Perhaps it should be mentioned here that a degree is an angular measurement, and that a complete circle contains 360 degrees.

The spark at the plug, and consequently the explosion, is so timed that the full force of the burning and expanding gases shall exert pressure on the piston immediately it passes the top dead-centre, but not before. Therefore when the engine is running fast the spark must occur before the piston reaches the top, because the burning of the gas, though very rapid, takes an appreciable time. If the explosion takes place too late the gases are still burning when they pass the exhaust valve, power is lost, the valve is damaged, and the exhaust port and pipe made very hot.

The exhaust valve is opened about 45 degrees from the bottom of the explosion stroke. A certain amount of pressure upon the piston is of course lost by opening the exhaust valve when only six-sevenths of the stroke has been completed, but the balance of advantage is in favour of this, for it gives more time for the exploded gases to escape. Lastly, the exhaust valve closes as the inlet opens, or on some engines just afterward, so that both valves are slightly open at the same time for a moment; but the momentum of the gases rushing down the exhaust-pipe, as already explained in connexion with the inlet pipe, helps to draw away what is left of the exploded gases in the cylinder head.

Timing-Gear of Twin-Cylinder B.S.A.

As the impulse acquired by the engine in one stroke, and that not a full one, has to carry it over three other strokes, and as it meets with most resistance in the last of the three, the compression stroke, a heavy fly-wheel, is a necessary part of an internal combustion engine. The valves are opened at the proper time by cams driven by the timing gear and closed by springs. As each valve opens and closes once during two revolutions of the engine the cams rotate at half the speed of the crank-shaft. Between the cams and the valve stems are interposed short rods called tappets. These are adjustable to ensure that the valves shall have the correct lift.

The Two-stroke Engine.—A two-stroke engine has the same sequence of operations, already set out, as a four-stroke; but in the usual type both sides of the piston are utilized, and consequently the cycle can be completed in one revolution or two strokes, because two things are being done at the same time. For instance, a rising piston draws a charge of mixture from the carburetter into the crank-case and at the same time compresses the charge which has been transferred from the crank-case to the cylinder. The explosion takes place at the top of the stroke, as in a four-stroke engine, and the piston descending under the force of the explosion partially compresses the charge already drawn into the crank-case during the previous stroke. As the piston nears the bottom of the stroke, ports are uncovered in the cylinder walls, first the exhaust port, then the transfer port. As soon as the exhaust port opens the used gases begin to rush out through the exhaust-pipe, and when the transfer port opens the fresh mixture, which is partially compressed in the crank-case, passes rapidly into the cylinder, driving what is left of the exhaust gas before it. So that the fresh mixture shall not pass straight across the cylinder and out through the exhaust port, the piston top is made with a deflector, against which the mixture strikes and turns upward toward the top of the cylinder, while the other side of the piston top is sloped toward the exhaust port to guide the exhaust gases on their way. Even so, there must be a certain commingling of the used and fresh gases and some loss of the latter through the exhaust port.

The usual type of two-stroke engine is constructed upon the above principle; but some have separate cylinders into which the mixture is first drawn and where it is partially compressed.

It will be clear that the spent charge must get out of the cylinder and the fresh charge get in during the time that the ports are open at the bottom of the stroke, and this time is very short, though not quite so short perhaps as is generally imagined. The crank-shaft must turn through about 110 degrees between the opening and closing of the ports, and this means that the engine passes through nearly one-third of a revolution as compared with a little more than half a revolution allowed for the entrance of the charge on a four-stroke engine. When the engine is turning at 1800 r.p.m., which is equivalent to a road speed of between twenty-five and thirty miles an hour depending upon the gear ratio, the gases must get in and out in one-hundredth part of a second, and as the velocity of gas under pressure is very high, this is quite within the range of possibility.

A two-stroke engine has the advantage of having no valves and no timing gear. It is in fact simpler than a four-stroke in construction, though not in design. It has twice as many power strokes in the same time, when running at the same speed, and size for size it gives about the same power. A four-stroke engine is faster, but a two-stroke has the virtue of pulling very well at low speeds.

It would be possible to make a six-stroke engine (and this has been advocated by some), the fifth and sixth strokes being utilized to draw in and expel a charge of pure air, thus scavenging the cylinder of all exploded gas and making the next charge more powerful. This would mean a heavier engine for its size, and one that would be somewhat harsh in action, so that it is not likely to become popular.

The Barr & Stroud Sleeve-valve.—It is usual for four-stroke motor cycle engines to have poppet (or mushroom) valves, and these have been referred to as being opened by cams and closed by springs. There is, however, at present on the market a single sleeve-valve motor cycle engine made by Messrs Barr & Stroud under the Burt-McCallum patents on the same lines as the engine of the Argyll car. The sleeve is operated by a half-time wheel having a special joint engaging with a pin that projects from an extension at the bottom of the sleeve. This produces an up-and-down motion combined with a partial rotation of the sleeve, the whole result being that any point on the sleeve describes what may be called an ellipse on the cylinder wall. This movement is utilized to open the inlet and exhaust ports in their proper sequence. The sleeve does not stop and start again, but continues to move all the time the engine is running at an almost even rate. This causes the engine to run with great smoothness and an absence of noise.

The piston operates inside the sleeve, and as the rotating movement of the sleeve is greatest when the piston stops for a moment at the top of the cylinder, motion between the two surfaces does not cease at that point but only when the piston is at the bottom dead-centre. The double movement of the sleeve has the advantage in distributing the lubricant very evenly and quickly over the surfaces in contact, as anyone may test for himself with a drop or two of oil between two pieces of glass.

At the moment when the explosion takes place the ports in the sleeve are above a junk ring (which is like a piston ring) situated in the head; the combustion space is therefore devoid of all irregularities, and can be made the best possible shape for efficiency. Also the shape of the ports causes them to be opened very rapidly so that they are equivalent to poppet-valves with a very rapid lift; but, unlike these, they are not noisy.

Messrs Barr & Stroud are the inventors and manufacturers of the range-finders used in the Royal Navy, which give a wonderful degree of accuracy over distances exceeding fifteen miles; therefore the accuracy required in a sleeve-valve engine, which is very great, is a simple matter to them. The Barr &

Stroud is at present made in three sizes, two singles of 350 c.c. and 500 c.c., and a twin cylinder of 1000 c.c.

The Bradshaw Oil-cooled Engine.—Internal combustion engines are for the most part cooled in two ways, by air impinging on fins cast around the cylinders, or by water contained in jackets which are also part of the cylinder casting and connected by pipes with a radiator carried in front and kept cool by the air circulating through it; sometimes a fan is also used behind the radiator, and this maintains a draught while the car is standing. Thus, although the manner of its application differs, in both air-cooled and water-cooled engines the ultimate cooler is the atmosphere.

Some few years ago Mr Granville E. Bradshaw decided to employ oil as the cooling medium between the cylinder and the atmosphere, and built both car and motor cycle engines on this principle. The cylinder has no fins and is let into the crank-case as far as the detachable cylinder head, which carries the overhead valves and rocker gear to operate them, and is finned to be cooled by air. At the base of the crank-case is a large sump containing oil, which is thrown by the crank-shaft upon every part inside the crank-case, lubricating the bearings and cooling the cylinder. The sump is ribbed, so that the oil in it is cooled by the air as the motor cycle rushes through it. This means that the engine is very thoroughly lubricated; but it does not use more oil than others, and not so much as a large number, because special precautions are taken to prevent the oil from leaking out or passing the piston to be burnt in the cylinder head and to cause carbon deposit. A large proportion of the oil used in many engines is either burnt or wasted in leakage; but it is essential in the Bradshaw engine that these sources of waste should be stopped or they would give endless trouble, and this is carried out very well.

Other Notable Engines.—Another engine designed by Mr Bradshaw is also worthy of special mention. This is the A.B.C., and it was the first engine designed since the War in the light of what had been learnt in aeroplane practice. It has steel cylinders bored from a solid bar with very fine fins turned upon its surface. The head is detachable and of cast-iron; both the valves are overhead and operated by push rods and rockers, the pistons are aluminium alloy. Ball and roller bearings are used throughout the engine and gear-box, except for the gudgeon pins, upon which the connecting rods rock in the pistons. The fly-wheel is not in the crank-case (this is usual with flat twins, which is the common name for engines having their cylinders horizontal and opposite to one another), but enclosed in a separate case to which the gear-box is bolted. This is very usual car practice nowadays, but though excellent it is very unusual on a motor cycle.

The Scott twin-cylinder two-stroke is also more or less unique. There have been other twin-cylinder two-strokes, but the Scott is the only one that has achieved any great degree of popularity and remained with us. This is doubtless for the reason that it is right in principle, which the flat-twin two-stroke is not. The two cylinders are side by side, and the cranks set at an angle of 180 degrees, that is to say, they are in a straight line. This arrangement gives good balance, and in a two-stroke engine even-firing intervals, so that the Scott engine runs like a four-cylinder car engine. On a four-stroke engine the firing would be very uneven if it were arranged in this way, a short interval followed by a long one. The Scott is water-cooled, and here again it differs from others; it is also capable of pulling a very high gear, and is well known for its speed and power.

Balance and Torque.—Reference has been made to balance; but it is not necessary to go deeply into that question. It is usual to balance a motor cycle engine by weighting the fly-wheels (when they are inside the crank-case), or by placing bob weights on the main shaft opposite to the crank pins. There is no simple method of balancing reciprocating masses by means of rotating ones, therefore all balancing of single-cylinder motor cycle engines must be in the nature of a compromise. If only the rotating masses were balanced by the added weights there would be left a large vertical unbalanced force, and if the weights were made equal to the rotating and reciprocating masses, then there would be an equally large unbalanced force in a horizontal direction. It has consequently been found best to make the added weights equal to the whole of the rotating and half the reciprocating masses. This leaves a much smaller unbalanced force in both directions.

In multi-cylinder engines it is easy to attain to great perfection in balance. A flat-twin engine is by nature almost perfectly balanced, since its pistons and connecting rods are always moving in opposite directions and balance each other without the addition of weights; a slight couple remains because the cylinders are not placed exactly opposite to each other. The Scott type of engine is balanced almost as well but has a slightly larger couple because the axes of the cylinders are farther apart. A vee-twin engine, which has both its connecting rods working on the same crank pin, one of them being forked and the two cylinders in line, can be well balanced, and the nearer the angle between the cylinders is to 90° (or a right angle), the better the balance will be. A 90° engine can be almost perfectly balanced, but its torque is not so good as when the angle is smaller, consequently in motor cycle practice the angle is generally about 50° or 60°; but 90° engines are used on light cars and cycle cars.

The Douglas, Coventry Victor, and A.B.C. flat-twin engines have equal firing intervals and consequently fairly even torque (torque is the turning effort of an engine, and if the turning effort were absolutely constant, then the torque would be even), and a firing stroke takes place at intervals of 360° or one complete circle. A single cylinder has, of course, equal firing intervals, one for every 720° if a four-stroke, or 360° if a two-stroke. A vee-twin with an angle A between its cylinders has alternate firing intervals of 360° + A and 360° − A. If a vertical twin four-stroke engine is designed to have equal firing intervals it must have its crank pins side by side, and its balance is then equivalent to that of a single-cylinder engine.

*Ricardo-Triumph 4-Valve
Engine with Masked Inlet Valves*

*Showing the Long Ball-Socket, Tubular Push-Rods and
Overhead Rockers Mounted on Rust-Proof Roller Bearings.*

Valves and Valve Gear.—It has already been explained that the type of valve used on four-stroke engines is that called the poppet, or mushroom, valve. These generally have seatings cut at an angle of 45° to the valve stem; but sometimes flat seatings are used instead. Occasionally, with the object of obtaining a very quick opening without undue noise, the valves are masked; that is to say the whole valve-head is let into the cylinder so that the opening does not at once become effective when the valve is lifted off its seating although it ceases to be quite gas-tight. By the time the valve clears the pocket into which it drops it has acquired a certain velocity and consequently the effective opening is quick.

To make a valve gear silent it must be so designed that the valve begins to open slowly, then gets quicker, and finally closes slowly. Valves designed to operate in this way have a smaller effective opening and are not so efficient. Therefore when engines are designed for racing, the valves are given a quick lift by making the cams steep; this is effective but noisy, and the masked valve makes a good compromise.

Valves may be placed at the side of the engine or in the cylinder head. The latter are the more efficient and give about fifteen per cent, more power in the same engine; but they are also more noisy. This is partly because of the extra joints required for the rocker gear, which is often unenclosed and difficult to keep well lubricated, and partly because, when an engine with overhead valves operated by push rods becomes hot, the gaps between the valve stems and rockers become greater. With side valves the reverse takes place, and a gap of about 1/64th of an inch is allowed when cold; as the engine warms up this closes, and the adjustment becomes just right. An overhead valve engine cannot be treated in this way because the tappets would have to be set so that the valves did not close when the engine was cold and consequently the engine would not start.

Sometimes an overhead cam-shaft is used; this is admirable in every way except that it adds height and complication to the engine.

On many engines, chiefly Swiss and American, the inlet valve is placed overhead and the exhaust at the side. On the pre-war A.B.C. this was reversed and the exhaust placed over, which had the advantage of keeping the hot exhaust gases away from the cylinder.

One advantage of both these arrangements is that the cool

incoming mixture impinges upon the hot exhaust valve and helps to keep down its temperature.

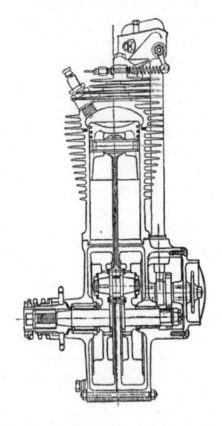

Section of the B.S.A. Overhead Valve Engine

Engine Lubrication.—For some time on a few British engines, *e.g.* the 3-h.p. Enfield, and on most American, to wit, the Indian, Harley-Davidson, Henderson, and American Excelsior, a mechanical pump has been used for lubrication purposes. This, when once set, requires practically no attention and is a great advance on the methods previously used in England, which were, first the hand-pump, then the drip feed operated by (1) a pump pulled up or pressed down by the rider and returned by the pressure of a spring, or (2) the suction produced in the crank-case of an engine when the piston rises to the top of the cylinder. This suction, or reduced air pressure, is maintained in the crank-case by the air being allowed to escape through a release valve as the piston descends; but the valve does not allow air to enter. This not only checks the blowing-out of oil through the joints of the engine, but produces sufficient suction to draw oil from the tank through a drip feed controlled by a needle-valve into the crank-case. Both these systems are good, but the mechanical pump, being positively driven by the engine, is better.

Sometimes a pump is connected up with the throttle so that as the throttle opens and more gas is supplied to the engine, which therefore does harder work, the oil supply is increased in proportion to the work done instead of in proportion to the speed of the engine. An engine running at a high speed downhill requires less oil than when it is climbing at a much slower pace under a heavy load.

When the oil is once in the crank-case, motor-cycle engines depend chiefly upon splash for the distribution of the oil to the cylinder walls and bearings; but some engines have ducts and passages through which oil runs to the parts which need it most. The oil in the crank-case of a motor cycle is churned up by the rapidly rotating crank or fly-wheels till it forms an oil-mist which reaches every part. Some parts, of course, do not need it but this cannot be helped. From the crank-case some of the oil passes into the timing-case where it lubricates the timing gear and cams, and then to the transmission that drives the magneto. There are one or two engines in which the gear-box is attached to the crank-case, forming a single unit, and the gears are then also supplied with oil from the engine.

CHAPTER IV

CARBURATION AND IGNITION.

VERY closely allied to the engine are the instruments which perform the duties of carburation and ignition. In fact the engine, magneto, and carburetter are often included in one phrase and called the power unit. The carburetter is, as its name implies, an instrument that carburets the air entering the cylinder of the engine—that is to say, impregnates it with a sufficient amount of carbon gas from the fuel to make a highly explosive mixture; and the magneto is a magneto-electric machine capable of producing a high-tension electric current which jumps across the plug points in the form of a spark and ignites the mixture in the cylinder at the proper time.

These two functions are very important, for the correctness of the mixture of gas and air has considerable effect upon the force of the explosion (air is itself a mixture of gases, but in this connexion the word 'gas' is taken to mean the gas vaporized from the fuel by the carburetter and mixed with the air that is passing into the engine), also the timing of the spark, already mentioned in Chapter III, and its hotness, make a considerable difference to the power developed.

The Carburetter.—At the present time a spray carburetter is the only type in use. The simplest form of carburetter consists of a pipe through which air rushes into the engine. This pipe is contracted for part of its length to form a choke-tube, and in this choke-tube is placed a jet from which petrol (called in France 'essence' and in America 'gasoline') issues in a fine spray. As has already been explained the descending piston draws air into the cylinder by suction. This really means that the piston creates a partial vacuum, which is filled up by the air in the induction pipe under the influence of atmospheric pressure; the partial vacuum extends into the carburetter and causes the fuel to be driven quickly through the tiny jet orifice into the choke-tube, where the rush of air vaporizes more completely, so that by the time it has reached the cylinder and been compressed it forms a homogeneous mixture. In the cylinder the mixture is whirled around owing to its rapid entrance; this is known as 'the turbulence of gases' and has much to do with their rapid burning, or explosion.

The simplest carburetter is, then, a jet in a pipe, and to this is generally added a float chamber containing a needle-valve operated by a float which allows the fuel to pass from the tank in the correct quantity to maintain a constant level, and a shutter to control the admission of air. Such a carburetter has two levers, one to control the admission of air to the carburetter—this varies the richness of the mixture and it is called the air lever; the other and more important lever controls the throttle and the quantity of gas and air mixture supplied to the engine. Most motor cycle carburetters have two levers, while car carburetters are generally of the single-lever type.

The reason for this is that it is a simpler matter to make an automatic carburetter—that is to say, one controlled by a single lever—for a multi-cylinder engine which is kept running at a fairly constant speed than for a single-cylinder motor cycle engine run at a constantly varying speed. There are many things to consider when designing an automatic carburetter, and a great many compensating devices have been invented to keep the mixture constant at all speeds and throttle openings.

It would be a simple matter to make the throttle admit more air and at the same time increase the jet-opening to admit more petrol in the proper proportion. This is done by attaching a tapered needle to the throttle barrel, which moves in and out of the jet as the throttle closes or opens and so keeps the mixture correct so long as the speed remains the same. But this is not sufficient, for it has been found that, as the velocity of the air through the choke-tube increases, it not only draws more petrol from the jet but more in proportion to the air, so that the mixture becomes richer.

It is now that the extra air lever is required, for when this is opened air passes more easily into the carburetter and the suction on the jet is lessened. Compensation can be made for this also by placing the jet away from the main air stream and by cutting passages in the carburetter to equalize the pressure or by placing the jet in a small tube. Sometimes several jets are used, one of which is often submerged, and when a proper selection of sizes has been made very satisfactory results are obtained.

Carburetters are generally made by firms who specialize in that work rather than by the makers of the motor cycle, and all these firms issue booklets describing their own particular instrument in full detail. American motor cycles are more generally fitted with automatic carburetters than British machines, and the Schebler is a very popular example. In England the Amac, B. & B., Binks, Claudel-Hobson, Cox-Atmos, Mills, and Senspray are largely used and give very good results.

One or two carburetters have no float chamber, but these are not much used. A float chamber consists of a small chamber into which petrol runs from the tank. When it reaches a certain level the orifice is closed by a needle-valve, lifted or pressed down by a hollow float made of thin copper. The petrol can be fed into the float chamber at either the top or the bottom. Both systems have advantages of their own, and the choice between them is merely a matter of taste.

The Magneto.—Ignition used to be one of the troublesome things about a motor cycle, but the high-tension magneto has entirely displaced the coil and accumulator in motor cycle practice and brought about a great change; ignition troubles are now rare so long as water is kept out of the magneto.

A complete knowledge of the principles of magnetism and

electricity governing the construction of a magneto is not necessary for the running of a motor cycle, but it is well to know roughly how a magneto is made and how it works. As may be expected, there is more than one type; that in most common use has a rotating armature between fixed magnets. The magnets, of which there may be one or several, are made of a special steel alloy. That used at present is three times more powerful than that employed before the War. At the ends of the magnets are pole pieces between which the armature rotates. The pole pieces are generally laminated—that is, made of many thin sheets riveted together, as this method of construction renders them more effective than solid blocks. They have curved faces which just clear the armature.

The armature consists of a piece of soft iron, round which are wound two coils of wire; the primary winding is made up of a moderate number of coils of fine wire, and the secondary coil of a very large number of coils of very fine wire. The former is connected to the contact-breaker and condenser, and the latter to the sparking plug. The contact-breaker is secured to the armature and rotates with it; the points are made of platinum, one is fixed and the other is carried on a spring or movable arm, and they are made to separate at the correct time, and at this moment the spark occurs at the plug. The condenser is a small packet of tin foil and mica in alternate layers, into which the current rushes when the points separate; its object is to prevent sparking at the contact points and to store electricity for the next spark. It has also the advantage of causing a more sudden break in the primary current and this helps to give a better spark.

Now a few words as to the why and wherefore. A magnet, having the power to attract iron, is said to be surrounded by lines of force. When a wire is moved rapidly across these lines of force an electric current is caused to flow through it.

Contact-Breaker of M.l. Magneto, with Cover Removed

Now the lines of force pass between the pole pieces from the north pole to the south, as they are called, and they pass through the iron core of the armature or its wide ends rather than through the atmosphere. When the core is lying across the pole pieces the lines of force pass through its centre inside the windings, but when the core is in a vertical position then the lines of force pass across the ends. It is at the moment of change that the lines of force are cut by the winding and the current generated in the primary winding. At the moment when these lines are being cut with the greatest rapidity the contact points open and the primary current is broken.

When two wires are lying side by side and an electric current is passing through one of them steadily nothing happens to the other; at the moment when the current is broken (or started) a current is *induced* in the other wire, and when there are many coils every coil helps to take up the current and a high voltage is produced. This is what happens to the secondary winding of a magneto, and a high-tension current is caused to flow to the plug where it jumps the points in the form of a spark. This current is taken up by a carbon brush bearing upon a brass strip in the slip ring at the end of the armature and it lasts for a small fraction only of a second, but that is sufficient. This current returns through *earth*—that is, through the metal of the engine and frame to the magneto.

If the points of the sparking plug are set too wide apart so that the spark cannot jump across them, or if they become broken, with the same result, damage would be caused to the insulation of the armature unless a *safety spark gap* were provided to complete the circuit. This gap is made much wider than that between the points of the plug, which should be only about half a millimetre (.02 inches), because the spark can jump much farther in air than in gas compressed in the cylinder, and also because it is not desired that the current should take the alternative path except in case of necessity.

The contact-breaker points should be set to open .4 mm., and the rocker arm kept free on its peg. A fibre bush is generally used here because it does not require oil, and this sometimes swells in damp weather and sticks. A twist drill of suitable size makes a useful tool to set this right; it should be turned backward while being inserted, so that cutting edges shall not damage the bush, and then turned the other way: no drilling-machine is needed as the drill can be rotated between the fingers and very little work is required. The platinum points should be kept clean and flat; but platinum being a very precious metal (costing about £20 per ounce), a file should be used as little as possible, gentle tapping with a light hammer will generally meet the case.

So far reference has been made to the most usual type of magneto in which the armature rotates, but it is possible to obtain the same results by rotating the magnets as is done in the B.L.I.C., in which the principle of working is practically the same. There is also another type of magneto called the 'Polar Inductor.' In this the armature and magnets are stationary, and a reversal of the lines of force passing from the north to the south pole of the magnets is brought about by a rotor or polar inductor provided with two shoes; one is in connexion with the north pole and always receives flux from it, the other conveys the flux to the south pole in whatever position they may be. The shoes are mounted on a non-magnetic metal, and as they rotate the flux passes through the windings, giving the maximum, then through the rotor, giving zero, and again through the windings, giving maximum in the other direction. The current is built up in either direction with great rapidity, and very good sparks are obtained—two per revolution.

By fitting more shoes to the rotor more sparks per revolution can be obtained, but two are sufficient on a motor cycle magneto. The axis of the rotor on these magnetos with regard to the magnets is at right angles to the axis of a rotating armature machine.

The range of advance and retard that can be obtained by rotating the cams around the contact-breaker is about 20°. A greater movement would cause the break to occur so far from the maximum position that only a poor spark would result.

CHAPTER V

FRAME-DESIGN AND CYCLE PARTS

MOST motor cycles are at present supplied with frames that are closely allied to the diamond frame of the pedal cycle. Certain changes have been made to fit this frame to its new purpose. There are two tubes at the top, and the tank is placed between them; the engine is bolted to brackets brazed to the frame-lugs, and completes the diamond part of the frame. Sometimes the central part of the frame is carried below the engine in the form of a loop, and this has the advantage that the frame is complete in itself and does not rely upon an aluminium crank-case to give it the requisite strength.

In a conventional motor cycle the gear-box takes the position occupied by the pedalling gear on a pedal cycle, but it is not often built into the bottom bracket. The usual method is to hang it below the rear stays by a couple of bolts sliding in slots so that a certain amount of backward and forward movement is allowed for chain adjustment. The engine is in front of this, and engine, gear-box, and rear hub are more or less in a straight line.

The front of the machine is supported on spring forks, of which there are a great number of different patterns; the most usual being adaptations of the Druid type, in which the forks are attached by links similar to those used on a parallel ruler. On some machines the main forks are rigid and the wheel is carried in links behind the forks, and the weight is supported on the axle by a supplementary fork and the necessary springs. American manufacturers favour this type. Another fork is pivoted below the head so that it can rock to and fro. The Triumph Cycle Co.,

Ltd., of Coventry, stuck to this type for many years; it is neat and strong, but has the disadvantage of altering the length of the wheel-base, as it gives to bumps on the roads.

Many motor cycle frames are duplex and thereby gain much in rigidity. These double frames are often made with a large loop or cradle in which both the engine and gear-box are placed. This is a very good form of construction and has much to recommend it. An excellent example of this is the 3 h.p. A.B.C., designed soon after the War (*i.e.* early in 1919). This frame is made unusually wide to protect the cylinder-heads and overhead valve gear of the flat-twin engine, which is placed across the frame. It also accommodates the fly-wheel containing the clutch, the four-speed gear-box, and the bevel transmission, above which the lighting dynamo is housed. This frame is wide enough to include comfortable foot-rests, and the whole mechanism, as well as the rider's legs, is protected by splash guards in front and rear.

The Scott is an early example of scientific frame-design. In this machine the engine, placed low down and well forward, forms the centre of the design, and straight tubes extend from this as required. There is no top tube, and the tank is mounted around the saddle tube. The weight is low down, and the machine steers and corners particularly well, as does, also, the A.B.C.

Among more recent machines to strike out a distinct line for themselves may be included the Cotton, Francis-Barnett, and P. & P. These are built almost entirely of straight tubes and are in consequence not only light but very strong and stiff. A stiff frame, especially at the rear, is most important on a very fast machine, and the big sports models made by several firms are reinforced with extra tubes for this reason. A frame that proves entirely satisfactory for touring may be, in spite of this, quite unsafe for racing with a very fast engine.

There is a feature in the Beardmore-Precision which is well worth mentioning: that is, the pressed-steel tank. This is stout enough to form an integral part of the frame; it is formed of two pressings welded together and to the lugs from which the frame tubes project. The little Premier twin two-stroke, now no longer in existence, was also made in this way. Motor cycle frames have been made almost entirely of sheet steel instead of tubes, but they have not up to the present been able to rival the more usual construction in popularity.

Straight tubes and triangulation certainly add to the strength and rigidity of a motor cycle frame; but that does not mean to say that a frame having a curved tube is badly designed. In some cases curved tubes are desirable, as, for instance, in the lower part of a loop frame where the curved loop below the engine certainly adds strength to the construction. Spring-frame machines, too, come under different principles of design. A strong and rigid point of attachment for the spring anchorage is of much more importance than a general stiffness.

Spring Frames.—The design and construction of spring frames for motor cycles is not so simple a matter as it might seem. In the first place, it is necessary to preserve the lateral rigidity, especially if the machine is designed for high speed; in the second, it is desirable that the distance between the centres of the chain sprockets should vary as little as possible; and in the third, the rising of the rear wheel over a bump, or its drop into a hollow, should alter the tension of the chain as little as possible. Spring-frame machines have been known to break their chains when passing over rough ground owing to the third point not having been properly considered. The first point demands that there shall be as few joints as possible, and that what joints there are shall be well constructed. The second point can be met by making the centre, about which the rear part of the frame moves, coincide with the centre of the sprocket on the gear-box, but this is inconvenient for constructional reasons, and if the pivoting joint is placed reasonably near this the variation in the distance will be very slight—so slight, in fact, as to be quite negligible.

Flat laminated springs, if placed correctly and well secured, will materially aid in preserving the lateral rigidity, and if these are combined with stiff forks properly hinged there need be little room for complaint on this score; but some of the old designs with many joints and sliding pieces left much to be desired. Quarter elliptic springs are the type generally used, and they are very suitable.

There is no doubt about the advantage of a well-designed spring frame; one has only to watch two machines, one sprung and the other rigid, passing over a piece of road to appreciate this, or, better still, to ride the two types, one after the other. However, in spite of their very obvious advantages, spring-frame motor cycles are not nearly so numerous as one would expect. This is partly due to the difficulties of construction already mentioned, partly to the extra weight (and it must be admitted that a spring frame adds considerably to the weight of a machine), and partly to the hardihood of motor cyclists in general, who are quite prepared to put up with an amount of bouncing and vibration that the occupants of cars would not tolerate.

An excellent example of the spring frame is to be found in the Indian. The rear of this machine is supported by two quarter elliptic springs with spirally curved ends. The springs are anchored below the saddle and pivoted to the rear part of the frame above the axle. The front is supported by a single laminated spring of the same type anchored beneath the head.

It should be noted, in passing, that it is desirable to synchronize the springing of the forks and the rear, and to use the same kind of springs. If long laminated springs are used in rear and helical springs in front, the two parts of the machine vibrate with different periods and the result is peculiar.

Another meritorious spring frame is the A.B.C. In the rear this machine is supported on two laminated springs which might be called double quarter elliptic. They are anchored at both ends, the main leaf runs from end to end, and the supporting leaves are above this in front and below in rear. The rear forks are in one piece and mounted on widely spaced roller bearings. The front springing is synchronized, and an ordinary quarter elliptic spring is used which is anchored in front and bears upon a roller below the head. This relieves that part of the frame of cross strains.

Many manufacturers have tried spring frames, often strongly resembling the Indian, but have not persevered in their manufacture. The Wooler frame is distinctive, the axles of both wheels press against spiral springs located in tubes. In the P.V. the rear wheel is carried in a rocking fork, supported in front by springs and hinged near the rear axle.

The introduction of the low-pressure tyres, which have proved so successful on light cars, to motor cycle practice is likely to hinder the production of spring frames, at any rate for some time to come; but a combination of the two would result in a very comfortable machine.

Cycle Parts.—The cycle parts of a motor cycle and pedal cycle differ in degree rather than in kind. The same things are used but they are much stouter and heavier. Larger balls are used in the bearings, more care is taken to keep out the dirt and retain the lubricant; sometimes Timken taper roller bearings are used instead of balls, and these make very fine bearings for hubs or head. The Brough-Superior has a beautifully designed head in which tapered roller bearings are used; these bearings will take both thrust and radial loads and are therefore ideal for the purpose. Thrust races are not correct for head bearings although often used. When a motor cycle is standing still its weight on the lower bearing is largely a thrust in its nature; but when the machine is in motion other stresses come into play, making the combination of a thrust and journal bearing necessary, and the Timken partakes of the nature of both.

Rims and spokes are also much stouter than on pedal cycles, and there is a tendency for the former to follow the light car rounded base pattern. Tyres have improved enormously of recent years. Most makers use a cord fabric, and the treads are very strong and will last for many thousands of miles.

Leather saddles stretched upon a frame have for some years

given place to shaped and padded saddles of fairly large size and well sprung. The latest innovation is the flexible topped saddle; this object being attained by placing the leather top over spiral springs, as in the Terry; aeroplane elastic, as in the Lycett; and flat strips of spring steel each supported by a small spiral spring, as in the Brooks. Those desiring still more softness in their saddles can fit a Moseley Float-on-air cushion.

Fast and powerful motor cycles are often fitted with steering dampers, little friction devices to check slightly the steering freedom of the front wheel. These, combined with shock-absorbers attached to the front forks, enable a machine to be steered steadily at speeds which without these appliances would be safe only for the most skilful riders. Steering dampers are also very useful on side-car outfits, the front wheels of which often have a tendency to wobble.

The brakes are very important items of a motor cycle's equipment; it will be readily understood that fast and heavy machines must have very efficient devices to check their speed. Ordinary cycle brakes have been found wanting and are now very seldom seen. The law enjoins the use of two independent brakes, and these should be fitted one to each wheel. Owing to the difficulty of fitting front-wheel brakes that are powerful and do not collect the mud, many manufacturers apply both brakes to the rear wheel. This is wrong in theory, and in practice a confession of weakness. A single rear brake is sufficient to lock the wheel and therefore a second brake on the same wheel cannot add to the stopping power, whereas a front brake can do so very materially.

A wheel should never be locked, not only for the very obvious reason that it is extremely bad for the tyre, and is very likely to cause skidding—a locked front wheel means an almost certain spill—but also because greater stopping power results from not quite locking the wheel. A sliding wheel loses some of its adherence to the ground, for the coefficient of friction between two surfaces decreases when these surfaces are moved one upon the other. This is proved also by the readiness with which a locked wheel will slip sideways on surfaces where a rolling wheel will show no tendency to slip.

Good and simple brakes are made by forcing a wedge-shaped block of fibre or some friction material into the vee of a belt rim. When chain drive is used a dummy rim is often fitted for this purpose, and a similar rim of smaller diameter can be used on the front wheel.

Internal expanding brakes of car type are also very effective as well as neat in appearance. Contracting band brakes are not so good and are apt to rub when not required.

It may sound like an anomaly but it is perfectly true that the absence of good brakes detract considerably from the speed of a motor cycle on average roads, unless one is prepared to take excessive risks. It may be argued that a man has a right to risk his own neck and his machine, but he most certainly has not the right to endanger the lives, limbs, and property of others. And this he does if he travel at high speed without adequate means of pulling up quickly.

There is another brake that should be mentioned which was designed for use in the Tourist Trophy races and patented by the Research Association. In this an inverted V-section ring, twelve inches in diameter, made of Fibrax or some other friction material, is attached to the wheel, and to this is applied an aluminium shoe having cooling ribs cast upon it. This is a reversal of the usual practice, for generally the brake block is made of some sort of fibre and bears in or around a dummy belt rim. The Research brake is very powerful, light, and wears well. As the fibre ring works against a soft aluminium alloy it has no tendency to glaze and lose its power, but it is essential that the ring should be true and firmly attached to the wheel.

CHAPTER VI

VARIABLE GEARS AND TRANSMISSION

ALTHOUGH the advantage of having the power to vary the ratio between the engine and the road-wheels is very obvious, it was many years before gear-boxes became universal. Now, however, every maker supplies motor cycles so fitted. For the most part the gear-boxes are supplied to the trade by manufacturers who specialize in their construction, but many of the large makers fit their own.

Some few motor cycle gear-boxes are precisely on the same lines as those fitted to cars, the gears being operated by sliding pinions. One pair of pinions is constantly in mesh, one being keyed to the lay shaft and the other free to revolve on the main shaft; when top gear is engaged this pinion is made to drive the main shaft by a sliding dog clutch and the lay shaft revolves idly. On the lower gears the drive is taken through the lay shaft and back again to the main shaft by the pair of pinions which operates the required gear.

It is usual to find three ratios on the bigger and better class motor cycles—a few have four speeds, and very nice they are, but three are generally considered sufficient—this means that there must be three pairs of pinions. A very usual plan is to have two pairs in constant mesh and operated by dog clutches, while the middle gears engage by sliding.

There is then a free engine position between top and middle and another between middle and low. As a rule only one of these is marked by a notch on the quadrant in which the gear lever works, namely, that between middle and low, as this is the usual position for the gear lever while the engine is being started.

In many gear-boxes the middle gear pinions are also in constant mesh, and this means that the two pinions must slide together, one on each shaft, and be engaged to their respective shafts as required by dog clutches. The advantage of this constant mesh idea is that the teeth of the pinions cannot be damaged while sliding into engagement by clumsy manipulation of the clutch and gear levers; the disadvantage is that it adds slightly to the complication of the gear-box.

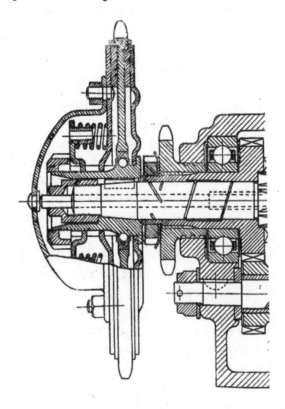

B.S.A. Dry-Plate Single-Disc Clutch

A four-speed gear-box on car lines gives one the power of changing from any one gear to any other without having to pass through the intermediate gears. This saves trouble when one stops with the high gear engaged and wishes to start in low. With a three-speed box it is necessary to pass through middle, and this may mean pushing the machine or turning the engine over to allow the gears to engage. It is not, however, a point of very much importance.

Most motor cycles are so arranged that power is applied to a gear-box and taken out on the same side, which means that the driven sprocket is mounted on a sleeve surrounding the main shaft. This plan is good as it has no tendency to cause the gear-box to twist and throw the sprockets out of line with their chains.

The clutch is usually applied to the driving sprocket of the gear-box, and this is possibly the most convenient place, all things considered, though it is more scientifically correct to place it on the engine-shaft, where the best place is in the fly-wheel. The speed here being about double the speed at the gear-box a similar clutch is about twice as effective, therefore it may be made much lighter. The gear-box clutch is, however, accessible.

Another type of motor cycle change-speed gear is the selective clutch. This is generally arranged to give two speeds only. Two chains drive from the engine to the countershaft, where either of the two sprockets can be engaged to the countershaft by expanding ring-clutches. One or other of these is expanded by a wedge and grips by friction on a drum inside the corresponding sprocket. The countershaft carries a sprocket from which a third chain runs to the rear hub. On a change-speed gear of this kind there is no engaging of dogs or pinions, and no separate lever for the clutch, so it is practically impossible to make a mistake in gear changing. When a lower gear is wanted nothing need be touched but the gear lever, which should be moved quickly across, and the engine will quicken up, during the moment it is free, to the speed required for the lower gear. In changing up it is better to raise the exhaust lifter, or close the throttle to decrease the speed of the engine during the moment of change, but it is not really necessary, especially if the clutch be put in slowly after it first begins to touch.

Hub gears have been tried on motor cycles, but in a hub space is very restricted, and they did not prove a complete success, although they answer well on pedal cycles. When a belt drive is used the hub is theoretically the right place for a change-speed gear, and a slipping belt may be cured by a drop to a lower speed, whereas if the gear were in the countershaft the slip would be made worse by similar tactics. This is because the belt is relieved of strain when a drop in speed is made between it and the road-wheel (the force applied at the road remaining constant), and its velocity increased.

Another method of varying the gear ratio when belt-drive is used is by opening and closing the flanges of the belt pulley and doing the opposite to the flanges of the belt rim to maintain the correct tension of the belt, as is done in the Rudge Multi, or by moving the back wheel to and fro, which is the plan adopted in the Zenith-Gradua gear. Variable pulleys are sometimes used alone, and in the Philipson pulley, which is varied automatically to suit the load by a heavy boss controlled by a spiral spring, the flanges are said to grip the belt and prevent slipping. A stouter spring may be used on this pulley to make the gear rise more quickly, in which case a low gear is obtained by pressing a small brake pad against the heavy boss.

The best-known gear-boxes are the Albion, Burman, Moss, and Sturmey-Archer. Four-speeds are found on the A.B.C., P. & M., and Rudge motor cycles. Enfield, P. & M., and Scott use the selective clutch gears.

One other type of varying gear should be mentioned, though it is not commonly used. This is the friction disc and wheel. This disc is of steel and driven by the engine; the wheel has a rim of fibre—specially prepared paper, or some other friction material—and slides upon a splined shaft. The nearer the wheel runs to the centre of the disc the lower is the gear; an infinite number of gears, between limits, can be obtained in this way; but in practice it is usual to notch the quadrant for about five ratios.

Transmission.—The subject of motor cycle transmission has already been touched upon while dealing with variable gears, for, gears being part of the transmission, the two are very closely allied. Belts are excellent for single-geared machines of the light sporting type, especially in fine weather; but owing to their propensity for slipping when the conditions are unfavourable and the load heavy, they have almost entirely given place to chains.

Chains naturally run best when properly enclosed in dust-tight cases and well lubricated, but even when run open and exposed to wet and dirt they are capable of wonderful mileages and very high efficiency. When run in an oil-tight case the best lubricant is of course oil, and engine oil is very suitable, but on an exposed chain oil is apt to collect the dust and form a grinding paste, which wears out both chains and sprockets. The best lubricant is then a mixture of grease and graphite. Price's Rangraphine, a mixture of Rangoon jelly and graphite, is very good—and the best way to apply this is to melt some of it in a flat vessel, such as a frying-pan, and immerse the chain, previously well cleaned in paraffin and dried, in it. The chain should then be moved about so that the melted grease can penetrate into all the links, taken out, and allowed to drain. The excess of grease can then be wiped off and the chain replaced. It is important that the grease should not be brought to the boiling-point or anywhere near it, since boiling grease is hot enough to draw the temper from steel; but it melts at quite a low temperature.

A chain should be adjusted so that it is in no position of the wheels actually in tension. Now it very seldom happens that a chain will be equally tight for all positions, therefore before adjusting a chain it is well to turn the rear wheel until the tightest spot is found and then adjust until there is a trifle of up and down movement in the centre of the chain-run—that is, half-way between the sprockets, and afterward test again to make sure that it is never really tight; a little too loose is better. When adjusting the chain of a spring-frame machine the wheel should be on the ground and a rider in the saddle. It is also necessary to see that the sprockets are truly in line and lie in the same plane. A little trouble spent on these points at home will be well repaid in smooth running and long life. Also it will very seldom be necessary to touch the chain when on the road, and this is a dirty job.

On some machines the primary chain, that from the engine to the gear-box, is the inverted-tooth type which is designed for silence and to take a certain amount of wear automatically by riding higher on the teeth of the sprockets. This is good because these chains will run satisfactorily at higher speeds than a roller chain will. Inverted-tooth chains are made by Hans Renold and the Coventry Chain Co. in England and several makers in America.

Chain-driven machines should have some sort of cushioning device in the rear hub. In addition to this, large machines and those with single-cylinder engines are generally fitted with shock-absorbing sprockets on the engine-shaft, but these are hardly necessary on small twin engines.

The four-cylinder Henderson has no primary chain, the first reduction being made by a bevel; this principle is also adopted on the A.B.C. The clutch in both these machines is correctly placed in the fly-wheel. In the Henderson the bevel is between the engine and the gear-box, in the A.B.C. between the gear-box and the rear wheel. This means that the A.B.C. has a lighter but faster running gear-box.

Shaft transmission has not yet come into its own in motor cycle practice. It is especially suitable for machines having four-cylinder engines and engines set with their crank-shafts longitudinal with the frame, as they are on cars. Universal joints make shafts quite suitable for motor cycles with rear springing, and this type of drive was used on the T.A.C., an interesting spring-frame four-cylinder machine, and the drive terminated in a worm. The F.N. has used shaft-drive satisfactorily for many years, and in this case a bevel is employed. On the latest F.N. models chain-drive is employed.

Although shaft-drive has not yet become as popular as it should be and will be in the future, enough has been done to show that it is entirely feasible. The appearance, too, is very neat since the shaft can be enclosed in one of the rear stays; all the mechanism is, of cource, enclosed and properly lubricated so that it wears extraordinarily well. When used with a single-cylinder engine this transmission is possibly a trifle harsher than a chain or belt; but this difference is not sufficient to be worth considering when there are real advantages to set off against it.

CHAPTER VII

PASSENGER MACHINES

VERY soon after motor cycles began to run on the roads it became clear that they might be made, by the use of a suitable attachment, to carry more than one person. In this connexion it was only natural for the trailer to come into use first. Roughly this resembled a light Bath chair with the front wheel removed and a curved bar substituted with a suitable attachment for fitting to the motor cycle below the saddle. It was fitted with a swivel joint so that it might tend to follow the curves in the road, allow the motor cycle to lean over at a corner, and also permit the trailer to keep both wheels on the surface of a sloping road while the motor cycle remained upright.

The trailer had certain advantages, *e.g.* it imposed no special strains upon the motor-cycle frame, it was partly sheltered from the wind by the machine and rider in front, though not sufficiently so to make any real difference to the power taken to draw it, and it was easily fixed and removed. On the other hand, the disadvantages were equally obvious after it had been in use for a short time. The passenger got the dust raised by the motor cycle wheels, as well as the exhaust gases, conversation was impossible and—most serious of all—the trailer was very easily overturned if a corner was taken too sharply or too fast, and it might be overturned by a bump on the road if the speed were high.

Another contrivance for the carrying of a passenger was the fore-car. This was sometimes made as a detachable fitment and took the place of the front wheel. The frame part was clipped to the frame of the bicycle, and the two wheels coupled up to the forks so that they could be made to steer. The fitting up, however, took much time and trouble, and fore-cars were generally turned out as complete vehicles to be used always as three-wheelers. The disadvantages were that the passenger was placed in front, and in case of a collision occupied the post of danger, and that the seat in front cut off the cooling draught from the engine and made it very liable to overheat.

Indian Super-Chief and Side-Car

These fore-car vehicles developed in time into the tri-car, and these in turn were made more and more elaborate until they became practically little three-wheeled cars, and larger engines were fitted. But the design was not really good, the frames were too weak for their length, and they presently died out. The nearest thing to these old tri-cars at present on the market are the Morgan and Harper runabouts, but these differ in many important particulars, and are thoroughly reliable vehicles. The Morgan especially has made a great name for itself in reliability and speed trials. This machine has its engine mounted, car fashion, in front between the two wheels and a single driving wheel. The Harper has one wheel only in front and the engine mounted at the side. Both of these, having three wheels only, are classed as motor tricycles and not as cars.

It would upon the face of it seem more reasonable to fix a passenger attachment in front or behind a motor cycle rather than at the side where it would cause side strains and the drive would no longer be in the middle. But it is true, though strange, that the side-car is a complete success although it would seem to be an unmechanical device. There have been various kinds of side-cars: one, the Lowen, had two wheels so that the complete outfit was a four-wheeled vehicle, the front wheel being coupled to the front wheel of the bicycle for steering purposes; another had its wheel near the centre of the body and attached to the bicycle wheel so that it moved through half the angle; a third type had a caster wheel which followed where it was led and needed no special alignment. Then there were the flexible types which allowed the bicycle to lean over at corners in the same manner as if ridden solo. These required the machine to be balanced just like a bicycle. One type of flexible side-car, the Appleby, had its wheel coupled to the bicycle wheel on the principle of a parallel ruler, and the width of the track did not change. This type was good and has been revived of late years in America. The other, in which the side-car wheel remained at right angles to the road and allowed the track width to vary, did not survive.

The rigid type of side-car is practically universal to-day; this is firmly attached to the frame of the bicycle at three, four, or five points. Sometimes it has a sprung wheel, but more often the chassis is rigid, and the body only supported on springs. This gives very comfortable riding; but when a side-car is attached to a machine with a spring frame, it is better that the side-car chassis should also be sprung by the addition of a spring between the chassis and the wheel if the full benefit of the springing is to be obtained, and preferably the side-car should be designed to suit the machine in the manner of its springing as well as in other ways. Good examples of this are to be found on the Matchless,

Beardmore-Precision, and A.B.C. machines.

The larger side-car outfits are generally sold as complete vehicles, and although the side-car is detachable it is not intended that the motor cycle and side-car shall be separated and the former used alone. They make very serviceable vehicles capable of considerable speed and good hill-climbing. It is often reckoned that a side-car outfit will carry as many passengers as can be piled on to it, and it is a common thing to see one on the saddle, two in the side-car, and another on the carrier with or without a pillion seat. Sometimes even five or six are carried.

Taxi-side-cars are used in some towns. In this case the side-cars are made wide enough for two people, and are enclosed. Tandem side-cars are also made for attachment to powerful machines.

Whether these big and powerful outfits will survive in competition with the cheaper type of light car or cycle-car remains to be seen. At present there does not seem to be any falling off in their popularity. They have the advantage of a lower tax and are slightly less expensive to run, but they lack the comfort of a car.

A.J.S. Twin-Cylinder Side-Car Outfit

The medium and low-powered side-car outfits are likely to increase in favour. At the present time even the smallest engines may be used with satisfaction to propel side-car outfits when suitably geared, owing to the great improvements that have been made in cooling. It was formerly impossible to gear low enough to enable a little engine to climb hills really well with a heavy weight, because the engine, travelling at a high rate of revolutions per minute, did not receive a sufficient cooling draught, when the machine was proceeding slowly, to keep reasonably cool. This difficulty has now been surmounted, and an engine of only 1 1/2 h.p. may be employed to carry two persons all over the country.

Then, too, it is often convenient to be able to detach the side-car and use the bicycle as a solo mount. And now we come to the proper alignment of the motor cycle and side-car, which is a matter of much importance if complete satisfaction is to be obtained. The big outfits are, of course, properly aligned by the makers; but side-cars fitted by the riders are very often wrongly fitted either through ignorance or carelessness. A very common sight on the road is a motor bicycle leaning over toward the side-car. This may be due sometimes to the connexions having slipped, but it is often done intentionally because the rider feels safer, especially when rounding corners with the side-car on the inside of the curve. It is, however, a mistake, and leads to bad steering and rapid wear of the tyres.

When the outfit is standing upon a piece of level ground the bicycle should be truly upright, and the side-car wheel should be in a plane very nearly parallel to the plane of the rear wheel. Theoretically the planes should be truly parallel, but in practice it has been found that excellent results are obtained when the side-car wheel points slightly inward to the front, and the side-car wheel is generally a little in advance of the rear wheel.

A side-car outfit has the advantage over the trailer and fore-car type in that it has two tracks only, and it therefore is not so shaken by a bad road because it may be steered so as to miss more of the pot-holes and bumps, and it is, upon the whole, easy to drive. Its weak point is, however, as has already been suggested, cornering. When the side-car is fitted as usual on the left of the machine there is a tendency for the outfit to turn over because so much of the weight is not within the wheel base; but it is easy to turn in that direction, and on a cambered road the camber should always be in the right direction. On a right-hand corner the disposition of the weight renders an upset less likely in spite of the fact that the camber generally slopes in the wrong direction; but the turning of the handle-bars to make the machine follow the desired course is often an actual physical effort.

A contrivance was used in the side-car T.T. race by F. W. Dixon, on his Douglas, to make cornering safer and easier. This was a lever working in conjunction with a sprung wheel so that the side-car chassis and body could be lowered while taking a left bend, and raised when turning to the right. This was certainly a step in the right direction; but this lever had to be operated by the passenger, and it is better that such action should be entirely automatic. It is, however, a great advance upon the practice of side-car passengers leaning out almost on to the ground to preserve the balance, and though hardly suitable for general use on the road it is excellent for racing purposes in the hands of experts. A sprung wheel alone increases the tendency to tip in the wrong direction at corners and makes more care necessary. The parallel ruler type of side-car, which leans automatically in the right direction, is really the best for fast work on winding roads.

CHAPTER VIII

ACCESSORIES, SPARES AND TOOLS

SOME motor cyclists equip their machines with a great number of accessories. This is unnecessary; but there are some things that are essential and others that are really useful. Among the essentials must be classed a lighting outfit, horn, certain tools, tyre inflator, and a repair outfit for tyres. The desirable things include speedometer and watch. It is also advisable to carry a few spares—for instance, a sparking plug, valve and spring, belt and fastener if belt-drive is used, otherwise a few spare links of chain. A belt punch or chain-rivet extractor should be included among the tools, and the tool kit should contain spanners to fit all the nuts on the machine, any keys that may be necessary, pliers, file, and punch. Mascots may be classed, for the most part, as foolish fads, though some few of them are ornamental and add a finishing touch to the machine.

Lamps.—Lighting outfits are now almost always electrical, and recent improvements have made these very satisfactory in use. It is desirable that these should contain a generator of electricity. Larger machines should have a dynamo to keep the accumulator charged, but on little single-cylinder motor cycles an arrangement to take some current from the magneto will suffice.

Lucas's Magdyno set has become very popular. This consists of a large magneto, the magnets of which are curved to allow of the insertion of a small dynamo giving five amps, and six volts. The two are separate electric machines, though mounted and driven together, and the failure of one will not affect the other. The Magdynette is a smaller machine on similar lines. On some machines the dynamo is mounted separately. The M.L. Maglita is a magneto of the polar inductor type combined with a dynamo. Other dynamo lighting sets are the Vandervell, P. & H., Miller, B.T.H., and Splitdorf. Then there is the B.T.H. Sparklight, taking the current from the magneto. The Villiers fly-wheel magneto also supplies current to the lighting set.

Battery lighting sets without a generator are also excellent and are supplied by most of the lamp manufacturers. When these are used the battery should be recharged at least every month, whether the lights are used or not. This is not necessary when a dynamo is fitted, as the battery is being recharged all the time the lights are in use; it should also be kept on charge during part of the daylight riding—say for the first hour on each ride.

Acetylene lamps give an excellent light, but are naturally a little more trouble than electricity. Dissolved acetylene gives the surest light and is clean, but the charged cylinders cannot be obtained everywhere. In connexion with acetylene there is a lamp called the Fallowlight in which, as in lime-light, the flame impinging upon a small sphere causes it to become incandescent and give a very steady light. All lamps require suitable reflectors to concentrate the beam ahead. In foggy weather a better riding light can be obtained by throwing this out of focus, or by pointing the lamp downward.

The part of an electric lighting set which is most likely to give trouble is the accumulator (or battery), and this should be examined from time to time, filled up with acid mixture, if any has been spilled, or distilled water if the loss is due to gassing, till the plates are covered; and it should never be allowed to remain discharged longer than can be helped.

When a dynamo lighting set is fitted, an electric horn may be added to the set, otherwise a bulb or mechanical horn is best, for an electric horn takes a considerable amount of current.

Speedometers.—Several principles are employed in the construction of speedometers, the most common being the centrifugal. In this a wheel with a heavy rim is mounted so that it can swing upon a shaft, and when at rest a spring keeps it in an oblique position relative to the shaft and the recording needle at zero. As the shaft rotates the centrifugal force tends to make it assume a position at right-angles to the shaft, and as the speed increases it compresses the spring and moves the needle round the dial, thus recording the speed. The Smith, Watford, and Jones speedometers are examples of this type.

Then there is the magnetic speedometer in which a revolving magnet tends to carry round a magnetic disc carrying the needle, of which the Stewart and A.T. are examples. The Cowey is operated somewhat on the principle of a wheel being made to revolve by quickly repeated blows of the hand, the more rapidly the blows follow upon one another the farther the wheel turns.

In all these the needles point all the time more or less steadily to the speed at which the motor cycle is travelling, but there is another instrument, the Bonniksen, which works on a principle called the isochronous. This is provided with an escapement like a watch which, while the machine is running, divides the time into intervals of half a second and four and a half seconds alternately. During the half second a needle is engaged by a clutch and travels forward a distance depending upon the speed; it then remains stationary for four and a half seconds. Then the second needle moves forward in the same way until it in turn records the speed and the first returns to zero. The speed is thus recorded every five seconds; some later instruments record every two and a half seconds. In another model, the Bonniksen combines a speedometer with a clock that works only while the motor cycle is running. Thus the actual running time can be read off without the trouble of timing stops and the average speed obtained, for every speedometer is also a distance recorder.

Carrying Tools and Spares.—The safe carriage of tools and spares is a matter which requires care but at the same time presents no difficulty. If put loosely into a bag or box they will rattle and be spoilt by knocking one against the other. Spare bulbs for the lamps should have a special receptacle; more substantial articles will travel safely if tightly wrapped in rags and packed closely. Any delicate article of luggage, like a camera, is best slung over the rider's shoulder and not carried on the carrier, but it would be safe in the side-car with a passenger.

If a watch is carried on the handle-bar that type is best which has the winder at the bottom; a luminous face is to be recommended, and a second hand is desirable if one wishes to take the time up a certain hill or between milestones.

It is sometimes advisable to have a spare tyre-cover and tube (on a side-car machine it is not unusual to carry a spare wheel complete, but this is not convenient on a solo mount). The tube can be wrapped round the handle-bar with the valve outside, all the air having been carefully squeezed out first, and secured by rubber bands; but a special case is of course neater. A cover is an awkward thing to carry, but it may be turned inside out, doubled, wrapped round the tank, and secured with a strap.

There are some few things which are often accessories but should really be part of the machine—for instance, splashguards. These are sometimes fitted by the makers of the machines as standard, sometimes as an extra; but often they are bought from the accessory houses. They are certainly necessary to all-weather riders, and protect the legs from the mud which drops from the front mudguards. An underscreen is another example. Some people carry the idea of protection against the elements very much farther and fit windscreens on their handle-bars and body shields on the front part of their frames. But motor cyclists in general are a hardy race and do not require these luxuries.

CHAPTER IX

DRIVING AND UPKEEP

THE driving of a motor cycle is now a very simple operation. This was not always the case, but improvements have been very rapid and have resulted in the simplification of the whole procedure. It is no longer difficult to find the correct mixture of air and fuel, for, although two-lever carburetters are the rule on motor cycles, they are so nearly automatic that they give even a novice very little trouble, and the same remark applies to the ignition.

Almost every motor cycle is supplied with a pedal, known as a kick-starter, with which to start the engine. The novice had better begin by putting the machine on its stand; but when experience has been gained a start can be made with the wheels on the ground, provided that the gear lever is in the neutral position.

Starting, then, with the machine on the stand, the ignition must be somewhat retarded, unless, as on some small machines, fixed ignition is used; the air lever must be closed, or, if the engine be hot, partly closed, and the throttle opened a little. Experience will soon show the best position for these three levers; it differs on different machines. No standard movement has been adopted for these levers, which is a pity; generally the air and throttle levers are mounted on the right handle-bar, the air above the throttle, and the ignition lever on the left bar. It is easy to ascertain by looking at the carburetter how the levers must be moved to open and close the orifices, but the ignition is not quite so simple. Therefore take off the contact-breaker cover from the magneto, turn the engine forward, and note the direction taken by the armature (it may be clockwise or anti-clockwise). Rotating the casing and the cams in the same direction by means of the ignition lever will have the effect of retarding the ignition. Full retard may result in a weak spark and, on the other hand, a fully advanced magneto may result in a back-fire. Therefore, follow the advice of Aristotle and strive to attain the happy mean.

One stroke of the kick-starter will rotate the engine several times, and the object to be aimed at is to make the engine pass through its induction and compression strokes and to the firing stroke rapidly, for thus a good spark will be forced to jump across the plug points, the charge will be fired, and the engine will start. To bring about this result, turn the engine over a few times with the exhaust-lifter raised; this will free the piston in the cylinder and make it move more easily. Then drop the exhaust-lifter and push the engine round till compression is felt. Raise the exhaust-lifter again and operate the kick-starter vigorously, dropping the exhaust again by the time the engine has completed half a revolution, which should be before the kick-starter is half-way through its stroke.

The engine should then start, but not at a great speed; when it is fairly on the move the air lever on most carburetters may be opened to its full extent, or nearly so, and the engine will quicken up a little and settle down to a steady 'purr.' With the gear lever still in neutral the rider can now take the machine off the stand and take his place on the saddle with his feet on the ground. The clutch must next be fully withdrawn and the lowest gear engaged, then as the clutch is gently let in the machine will move off. While letting in the clutch the rider should open the throttle; but both movements must be done gradually or one of two things will happen: either the machine will go off with a disconcerting rush or the engine will stop, and the whole process will have to be repeated. It is well for a novice to run a little while in bottom gear before changing up. This is done by closing the throttle a little, taking out the clutch, and moving the gear lever steadily and without undue haste into the required position. It can also be done by raising the exhaust valve lifter and moving the gear lever, but the first method is the more correct.

Motor cycle gears generally change so easily that there is no need to use the method of double-declutching, which is so useful on cars, when changing down. On some gears the lever can simply be pushed quickly across, and the engine accelerating when momentarily free will be running at the right speed for the lower gear by the time it is engaged. It is, however, generally better to take out the clutch nearly all the way to soften the change. When changing down, the throttle may be partly closed, but this should not be done so much that the inertia of the machine will drive the engine, as the engine must accelerate while the change is being made.

If the machine has no clutch a little more agility is required to effect a start; but it presents no real difficulty. Push the machine with the exhaust valve raised until the engine is turning over quickly. Drop the exhaust and the engine should start at once. If any difficulty is found in jumping into the saddle, the exhaust can be raised again for a moment to check the speed while the foot-rest is used as a step and the other leg thrown over the saddle. If the machine has more than one gear it will be found easiest to push off on a high gear, but to mount on a low. It is not convenient to use two gears in this manner, and if the machine has a three-speed gear-box, the middle gear is likely to be the best compromise. What is wanted is that the engine should be turned quickly with the least possible effort. If the low gear be used, the engine will certainly be turned quickly, provided that the machine can be pushed without the rear wheel sliding; but the effort required to push the machine will be proportionately greater. A high gear will, on the other hand, need a higher pushing speed.

The push start is often useful when an engine provided with a kick-starter proves refractory. In this case the clutch must be withdrawn when the engine fires, and the exhaust-lifter not touched, the gear is then put into neutral for a moment while the rider gets into the saddle, and a start made in the manner described above.

A motor cycle engine, especially one of the modern type which combines small size and high power, depends largely for its power upon its speed. It works by means of a large number of small impulses given in rapid succession. Horse-power is merely the rate of doing work, and an engine that can exert 550 ft.-lbs. per second is said to give one horse-power. One ft.-lb. is the work required to lift 1 lb. through a distance of 1 ft.; 550 ft.-lb. is therefore the work done in lifting 550 lb. through 1 ft., or 1 lb. through 550 ft., or, say, 55 lb. through 10 ft., and so on. Therefore, as the impulses of a small engine are but small they must necessarily be rapid—that is to say, the revolutions per minute of the engine (called shortly the r.p.m., or merely the 'revs.') must be high. If, therefore, the rider is desirous of getting the utmost out of his engine, he must keep up the 'revs.'

In the days when all motor cycles were single-geared keeping up the 'revs.' meant keeping up the speed of the machine, and if a hill could not be climbed fairly fast it could not be climbed at all. Engines varied then, as now, and some had the power of keeping steadily on, pulling well at a slow pace. These had large fly-wheels—sometimes outside the engine—and were known as the slogging type.

At the present time small engines capable of very high speed are in fashion, and it is possible to keep up the 'revs.' by using the gear-box. This means that the engine can be used as it should be and advantage taken of its power without the necessity for reckless riding, because bad hills can be ridden slowly instead of rushed.

It is quite a common thing to hear motor cyclists boasting that they have climbed such and such a hill on top, by which they mean that they have climbed it on their highest gears. There is no special virtue in top-gear climbing; unless it can be done easily it is bad for the engine as well as for other parts of the machine, and if a really steep hill can be climbed easily on top, it simply means that the gears are lower than they should be. A single-geared machine must, of course, do its climbing on top; but a single-geared machine with a belt-drive can be considerably lighter than one of the same power fitted with a gear-box and chain transmission, and its gear must be a compromise between what is required for speed and for climbing.

A gear-box is there to be used; there is no object in carrying useless weight. What is wanted in a motor cycle is ability to climb a hill with certainty and as fast as may be desired, not to climb it on top. A drop in gear when climbing a hill will often mean an increase in speed without any alteration to the throttle. Every engine has one set speed at which it gives its greatest horse-power, and the best gear on every hill is that which allows the engine to maintain this speed at full throttle. If the gear be too high the engine must slow down and consequently lose power, if too low it will increase its r.p.m., and again the power will fall below the maximum and the speed will not be so high as when the correct gear is used.

The following story will illustrate the point I wish to press home. One afternoon I had just commenced the ascent of a moderate hill, about half a mile in length, when the rider of a much larger machine overtook me. I was in no hurry and should probably have taken no notice of him but for the fact that by keeping too close he forced me to slow up behind a cart that we were overtaking. He then looked back and grinned, opened his throttle, put his head down and went away. I was riding an A.B.C. which has a four-speed gear-box. The hill was one that the machine would easily climb on top, but on this occasion I wanted more acceleration, so I dropped into third, opened my throttle about half-way, and passed my gentleman, who had got a lead of about fifty yards while I was held up by the cart, some two hundred yards or so before reaching the top of the hill. I shall not forget his look of astonishment, as I shot past him, for many a day. If I had kept the top gear engaged I could not have caught him in the time, but the lower gear made it quite easy.

My advice is therefore to make full use of the gearbox and to change gear in plenty of time, if it is desired to make a fast climb. If a sharp rise is known to follow a bad corner the novice will be well advised to lower his gear before turning the corner, for a bad corner must be taken slowly, and by dropping his gear before the corner he will be enabled to keep up his 'revs.' Even expert riders often make the mistake of trying to do things in too high a gear. For instance, in an account of the Colmore Cup trial it is usual to read, "Several riders made the mistake of trying to get off in the stop and restart test in second instead of using bottom gear." When approaching a rise that can be climbed easily on top speed, it is well to quicken up a little as one nears the hill. The gear-box is also very useful when facing a gale of wind on a level road. It is a great mistake to overdrive a motor cycle engine, and one form of overdriving is hanging too long on to top gear. For this reason I have emphasized the point. A motor cycle which is carefully driven will last very much longer and give better service.

If it is a mistake to over-drive a motor cycle at any time, it is doubly foolish when the machine is new. For at least two hundred miles a new machine should be driven only at a moderate pace. This gives the various working parts an opportunity of suiting themselves one to another, and the machine gets 'run in,' as it is called, after which a high speed does no harm.

There are many brands of oil on the market possessing excellent qualities. The oil makers issue lists showing which of their different brands are best suited to every machine on the market for summer and for winter use. These lists are well worth studying. It is also very well worth while to take the makers' advice as to the particular make of oil that should be used. Some engines run best on a plain mineral oil, others are best suited by a compound oil. When an aluminium piston is used an oil containing an admixture of castor oil is excellent, but not essential. For racing purposes a large proportion of castor oil is generally used. Castor oil is, however, unsuited to the lubrication of two-stroke engines by the method known as 'petroil,' which consists of mixing oil and petrol together in the tank in the proportion of 1 of oil to 14-16 of petrol.

Of late years upper cylinder lubrication has become popular. This is done by mixing 1 oz. of a special oil with two gallons of fuel. When using this the usual oil supply is continued, but a little less may be used.

While it is undesirable to use too much oil, as it results in a dirty engine and oiled plugs, which must be taken out and cleaned, it is better to use too much than too little, for this may result in seizure, overheating, distortion and serious damage. Oil is cheaper than new parts, and it is less trouble to clean an engine than to repair it.

Every engine requires to be decarbonized, or cleaned, periodically; some need it much more often than others, and it also depends upon how an engine is driven. Generally speaking, a large engine driven well within its power will run for a much greater mileage before cleaning is necessary than a small engine driven hard. Also a coating of carbon of a given thickness will make more difference to the compression ratio when the cylinder is small, for obvious reasons, and will therefore cause the engine to knock, or pink, more quickly. Knocking or pinking is a noise made by the engine like that made by a hammer on an anvil, and it is a sure sign that the engine needs to be cleaned, provided that the ignition lever is not too far advanced. Another sign is loss of power.

It is then necessary to remove the cylinder head or the complete cylinder, having first taken off the inlet and exhaust pipes. Removal of the cylinder head is sufficient for simple decarbonization, but the whole cylinder should be taken off now and then so that the piston may be cleaned on the inside where burnt oil is likely to accumulate and the gudgeon pin fixings inspected. At the same time it is well to examine the piston rings and see that they are free in their grooves and oily, but not loose enough to have any up-and-down movement. If the rings are free and a good fit there is no need to remove them, for a little carbon behind the rings is an advantage rather than not. If, however, a ring is stuck in its groove, it must be dislodged, and it is very difficult to do this without breaking the ring, as piston rings are made of cast-iron and are very brittle. If not very tight a ring may be gradually eased off, and a thin strip of steel inserted at the slot and pushed behind the ring will sometimes be a help; but great care is required.

To assist in putting on or taking off piston rings, it is well to provide oneself with three or four strips of sheet metal about a quarter of an inch in width and, say, a couple of inches long. These can be cut out of a tin and hammered to remove the roughness of the cut edge, and it is a good plan to turn over one end and fasten them loosely together with a piece of string half a yard long. If used singly they are very easily dropped into the crank-case, but not so easily fished out again. These bits of metal are inserted one by one between the piston and ring, and then slipped round until the latter will slide off. When reassembled the slots of adjacent rings should be on opposite sides of the piston.

When a cylinder is taken off, a piece of rag should be wrapped around the lower part of the piston, and the piston pushed down to the top of the crank-case. The rag will protect the piston from damage and prevent dirt from falling into the crank-case while the carbon is being removed from the top of the piston. An old file with its end suitably ground makes a good tool for this purpose, or a broken hack-saw blade may be used as a scraper; an old chisel or a long screw-driver may be used for the cylinder, care being taken not to scratch the walls. When this is done, all the bits of carbon and dust must be removed and the parts washed in paraffin.

It is likely that the inlet port will be found to be partially choked with a soft dirt, which will also accumulate on the back of the valve and on the stem. This is easily scraped away, but care must be taken not to damage the faces of the valve and seating. It is only occasionally that the inlet valve will require cutting or grinding, but the exhaust valve should have attention whenever the cylinder is taken off. The J. & S. re-seating tool is excellent for this purpose as it will quickly true up both the valve and the seating; the latter will need very little treatment. When grinding the valves with paste or powder, put a thin coating evenly all round the valve (too much powder or paste is not only wasteful but cuts more slowly), turn the valve backward and forward a few times, then lift it off its seating, replace in a different position, and repeat the operation. Grinding powder requires oil from the start; paste is all the better for the addition of a little oil as the operation proceeds. All traces of the abrasive must be washed away when the grinding is complete. Much grinding is apt to wear away the seating, and then the valve drops in too far and is pocketed, so that a certain portion of the opening is lost and the cylinder will then have to be sent to the maker for the seating to be re-cut. Some engines are designed with pocketed valves, the object being to obtain a quick and quiet opening; but allowance is then made for this in the timing, and a longer lift is given to compensate for the pocket.

When new piston rings are fitted it is desirable that they should first be tested in the cylinder. The skirt, that is, the lower part, of the piston should be used to push the ring some little way into the cylinder, as this will ensure its lying in a plane at right angles to the axis of the cylinder and not askew. When inserted in this way there should be a small gap between the ends of the ring, which may vary with the size and number of the rings. As much as 1.5 mm. may be allowed when there are three rings, but a smaller gap is generally preferred, about 0.5 mm. When an engine has had much wear the upper part of the cylinder is generally a little larger in bore than the lower part. This may be tested by noting the difference in the size of the gap when the ring is placed in different positions. The elasticity of the ring should enable it to make good contact with the cylinder throughout the stroke, in spite of a little difference in the bore.

Most of these operations may be carried out without removing the gudgeon pin and piston; but if it has been found necessary to remove these it is important that the gudgeon pin should be replaced as it was if it be a taper fit, and in any case it must be properly secured or its end will score the cylinder, and that will mean a job for Barimar Ltd., who can do wonderful things with their patented welding processes, as I have personally proved to my satisfaction.

CHAPTER X

TROUBLES ON THE ROAD

WHEN a motor cycle is well looked after at home, and the necessary adjustments properly made, it will only be very seldom that it requires attention on the road. If the machine stops after spitting once or twice through the carburetter, the cause is, as likely as not, to be nothing more than lack of fuel. It is then advisable to turn off the petrol at once and inspect the tank and carburetter. The latter may be empty when the former contains an ample supply, and then the obvious cause of trouble is a stoppage in the petrol pipe. This may not be detected at once, unless the petrol is turned off, because the fuel may run through slowly and refill the float chamber although it is not passing quickly enough to supply the needs of the engine. If there is petrol in the carburetter, a choked jet may be the cause of the trouble, and if the carburetter has a needle in the jet moving this up and down may clean it; otherwise the jet must be taken out and cleared, which can generally be done by blowing through it.

It is best to look first at those things which are most readily accessible, as this may save both time and trouble. Therefore the sparking plug may be examined before taking the carburetter down. A plug which is covered with burnt oil will not spark and must be changed or cleaned. When it is black with soot it indicates too rich a mixture and the remedy is obvious; but when in a twin-cylinder engine one plug is so covered and the other clean, it suggests an air leak in the cylinder from which the clean plug was taken and a general enriching of the mixture to obtain an explosion; and the air leak must be discovered and stopped. This may mean nothing more than the tightening of the inlet pipe; but air sometimes leaks past the valve guides and causes bad running at low speeds, firing in one cylinder only, and poor running. The fitting of Flexikas springs or Airtite washers will cure the trouble. Plugs are so reliable nowadays that they give no trouble for thousands of miles, but it is advisable to take them out occasionally and smear the threads with graphite grease, or it may be found well-nigh impossible to remove them when occasion arises.

If the plugs seem to be in good condition, test the spark by connecting the high-tension wire and laying the plugs on the engine. If there is a good spark the trouble is not likely to be in the ignition; but it must be remembered that a spark can sometimes be obtained in the open air when the plug will not spark under compression in the cylinder. Bad sparking with good plugs points to a fault in the magneto. The contact-breaker may require attention, as explained in Chapter IV, or the carbon brush which picks up the high-tension current and carries it to the plug and the slip ring in which it works may require cleaning with a piece of clean linen and a little petrol.

Sometimes a valve sticks in its guide and causes the engine to cease to function, it is then necessary to take out the valve and clean the stem. This trouble is more likely to be encountered at starting and is often caused by oil becoming burnt and stiff. A broken valve is very easily discovered, so is a broken valve spring. If the valve head can fall into the cylinder, as it can when placed overhead, it may do serious damage to the piston or cylinder; therefore any sudden noise or rattle in the engine should always be followed by an immediate stop, and no attempt should be made to run the engine until the trouble is discovered and removed.

So long as plenty of good oil is used there is not likely to be a seizure in the engine. A piston seizure will bring the machine to a quick stop with a grating or grinding noise; but it can generally be cured by a liberal dose of paraffin poured into the cylinder and the gentle movement of the engine by pushing the machine backward and forward. The paraffin will get into the crank-case and therefore the latter should be drained and a fresh supply of oil inserted before starting again.

The seizure of a bearing can generally be cured in the same way, but this time the paraffin must be poured into the crank-case, and to do this will not be particularly easy; the oil-pipe connexion is the most likely place. After the engine has been made fairly free, by a gentle movement it can be turned quickly before the paraffin is drained out. When a plentiful supply of fresh oil has been inserted, the engine should again be turned round so that the oil can work its way into the bearings before it is run under its own power, and for a time it should not be run at a high speed. The big end bearing is most likely to give trouble in this way, especially when it is a plain bearing of phosphor-bronze. A roller bearing is not likely to seize in the ordinary way, but sometimes a roller will turn sideways and jam the bearing, so causing a sudden stop. When this happens the engine must be taken to pieces, and it will very likely be found that a new crank-axle and connecting-rod will be required, as well as a new bearing. This is too serious a repair to be undertaken by the roadside.

Seizures are generally caused by the use of unsuitable oil, or by an insufficient supply. The cure for the former is to buy oil only in sealed tins and to use that brand recommended by the makers of the machine; if that does not happen to be available it is best to consult the list of any oil merchant whose product is stocked, and to choose the brand recommended in that list for the motor cycle in question. The remedy for the latter is obvious, *viz.*, give more oil; but the deficiency may be due to an obstruction in the pipes, which must in that case be cleaned. It is not likely that a mechanical pump will go wrong, but in very cold weather the oil may refuse to flow to the pump and a thinner oil be needed.

Most makers of repute issue little booklets of detailed

instructions concerning their machines, with hints for starting and running. Every purchaser should possess one of these and study it carefully, for all the advice given is the result of long experience.

CHAPTER XI

TOURING AND RELIABILITY TRIALS

THE true object of a motor cycle is to enable its rider to travel quickly, easily, and cheaply from place to place, and it certainly provides the cheapest form of mechanical transport for one, or two, persons. Except for short journeys which can be accomplished in a single day by the rider's own exertions, a motor cycle is a less expensive mode of travel than a pedal cycle; because it can easily double the day's journey and therefore halve the hotel bills.

To demonstrate this reliability trials have sprung into existence. Some of these are designed to show that great distances can be covered on good and moderate roads without undue fatigue, and others that a motor cycle can go anywhere where there is a road, no matter how bad, and to many places where no roads exist. It has long since been shown that no ordinary hill with a reasonably good surface is too steep for a motor cycle, and therefore the promoters of the latter kind of trial seek out steep hills which also have bad surfaces or difficult corners. Where failures occur, they are generally due to lack of grip for the wheel or bad riding.

The principal trials organized by the Motor Cycling Club, the London-Land's End trial at Easter, the London-Edinburgh trial at Whitsuntide, and the London-Exeter and back trial at Christmas time, belong to the former category. Of these the London-Edinburgh is the oldest and longest. The route used to be up the Great North Road through Grantham, York, Newcastle-on-Tyne and Berwick-on-Tweed to Edinburgh; but as motor cycles improved this route became too easy to be considered a good test, and a divergence was made over the Pennines and through the Lake District of Westmorland and Cumberland, for the sake of including some really steep hills, such as Kirkstone Pass, which is ascended from Ambleside, the most severe climb up this pass.

Bad weather is often the cause of the difficulties encountered in the London-Exeter, for it is held at a time of the year when fog and rain are not unusual. Sometimes heavy gales are met and the roads are often flooded in places. The trial starts in the evening of Boxing Day, and hills which present no special difficulties in the day-time may be hard to climb at night. Some severe hills near the Devonshire coast are included in the outward run and climbed in the dark. Other hills are taken on the return trip which also traverses the most hilly parts of Dorset. Partly because the days are short, this trial includes more riding in the dark than the other two.

The night riding in the London-Land's End trial is over fairly easy country, down the Bath road through Reading, Newbury, Marlborough, then by way of Trowbridge and Glastonbury to Bridgwater, where breakfast is taken. After this some of the steepest hills in the northern parts of Somerset and Devon, on the borders of Exmoor, are climbed. There is a timed mile on Porlock Hill, Countisbury Hill is descended (this makes a fine test for brakes, as the hill is steepest near the bottom and terminates in a sharp corner near Lynmouth harbour). Next comes a half-mile climb to Lynton, and very soon the ascent of Beggar's Roost, which is very soft and rough and so steep that it is said that a car will roll over if it is turned sideways. Many miles of rough going bring the competitors to Launceston, then over Bodmin Moor (rough near Bodmin), and to Perranporth, beyond which are narrow lanes and the last new test hill, Bluehills Mine Hill near St Agnes. A dangerous descent leads into the valley with a left-hand hairpin bend in the steepest part, then there is a right-hand turn to the bridge, which crosses the stream leading to Trevellas Porth, and a second right-hand turn off it. The test hill now commences. This has an average gradient of about 1 in 6 and a hairpin bend, again a left-hand one, on a gradient which is 1 in 3 on the inside and 1 in 5 on the outside. A middle course must be steered here or it is difficult to get round. From this point the coast road is followed to Hayle, the main road to Penzance, and narrow lanes to the finish.

Sporting B.S.A., of the Type that Ascended Snowdon

The six-days trial organized by the Auto-cycle Union, now known as the Stock Machine Trial, and the Scottish Six Days are undoubtedly the most important trials held, and they belong to some extent to both categories. The first is practically a trade trial, and the second a sporting event. The routes are varied from year to year and they are very strenuous. For the Stock Machine One Thousand Miles Trial A.C.U. representatives choose certain motor cycles from the stocks of manufacturers or agents, which are ready for sale to the public. These are handed over to the riders just before the trial for any little adjustment; but no great alterations can be made. This procedure ensures that special machines shall not be used for trial purposes which are different from those usually sold. The regulations are stiff and the trial carefully observed and a report issued covering every important point. This trial was first run from Land's End to John o' Groats, then around a certain centre, or centres, over a different route each day. Now the same route is used and covered in both directions.

The Scottish Six-Days Trial is a very sporting event, starting from Edinburgh and running into the Highlands, with sometimes a circular trip in the Lowlands on the last day. The hills are steep and long, the scenery magnificent, though the attention of the competitors is too much occupied with the road to give it the attention it deserves, and the regulations not too strict to make the trial enjoyable, and consequently it is very popular with amateur riders. The Pass of the Cattle is often included in the route, this lies between Applecross and Tornapress and is the only road into the former place. There is a steep ascent on either side abounding in bends and about five miles in length—a splendid test for engines and their cooling powers.

The two Midland trials, the Colmore Cup and the Victory Cup, and many other one-day trials, are designed to show that no road is too bad for a motor cycle. The Colmore Cup trial includes all the worst hills in the Cotswolds between Stratford-on-Avon and Cheltenham, and some of these are very steep and rough. The Victory Cup route lies for the most part to the south and west of Birmingham, over the Lickeys and Clent Hills, where many of the roads are merely rough tracks and water-splashes are common.

Trials of this sort soon find out the weak spots of motor cycles when they exist, and go far toward demonstrating to overseas riders that a motor cycle can go practically anywhere. The Scott Trial held annually in Yorkshire and mostly away from the metalled roads is also useful in this respect, as are the scrambles over the Surrey commons in which the Camberley Club delights. Some people seem to take a special pleasure in using things for purposes other than those for which they were intended, and in the case of motor cycles this has its uses, and the breed is improved thereby.

It was with the object of demonstrating to the world at large that a motor cycle could be usefully employed in most difficult country that B.S.A. Cycles Ltd. organized, in May 1924, the ascent by motor cycle of Snowdon. Under A.C.U. observation a 3.49 h.p. model ascended by the side of the mountain railway track in 24 min. 6 sec.; this is more than twice as fast as the ascent by a car and about one-third of the time usually taken by the train. A 2.49 h.p. model ascended in 30 min. 54 sec. Neither machine stopped by the way or received any assistance. This track has an average gradient of 1 in 5, and is about four and a half miles in length. The ride was one of considerable risk. In one place there was only about eighteen inches between the rails and a steep drop of a thousand feet. The weather was most unfavourable, a strong wind was blowing and a thick mist drifting across the track, and the riders could only see a few yards ahead.

Two 3.49 h.p. models made the ascent of the path the fastest, taking 41 min. 8 sec. This route was perhaps less dangerous, but more physical effort was required from the riders. The total length was about the same, but the gradient in places was as steep as 1 in 3, or perhaps a trifle worse, the surface was atrocious. Wheel-spin delayed the riders in a marshy place and rendered some outside assistance necessary; there was plenty of loose shale, over which it was not easy to *walk*, and near the top rocks jutted out and bent the foot-rests. The machines stood up to the test wonderfully well, and the engines developed plenty of power. On the next day, in beautiful weather, further ascents, this time unofficial, were made. Only four machines were sent up for the official tests so that a 100 per cent, success was scored.

Those motor cyclists who wish to tour in the British Isles (and who does not ?) should make a point of joining the Automobile Association and Motor Union, whose patrols are to be found all over the country and who will give useful information regarding routes, hotels, and the state of the roads, or the Auto-Cycle Union.

CHAPTER XII

MOTOR CYCLE RACING

THE sporting side of motor cycling consists of speed trials on the road, racing on the track, hill-climbs and, most important of all, the Tourist Trophy races and the Grand Prix races on the Continent.

It is probable that a remark made by the late H. Walter Staner, editor of *The Autocar*, at a dinner held by the Auto-Cycle Club (now the Auto-Cycle Union, and the ruling body of motor cycle sport), led to the inauguration of the Tourist Trophy races, generally called the 'T.T.'

Be this as it may, a trophy was presented by the Marquis de Mouzilly St Mars, and the first race took place in the Isle of Man over a triangular course fifteen and a half miles in length, having Ballacraine, Kirkmichael, and Peel at the corners, and the race has been held in the Island yearly since then, except during the War.

At first there was a petrol allowance of one gallon for every ninety miles to single-cylinder engines and one gallon for every seventy-five miles to twins. This naturally kept down the speed and was removed two years later. Pedalling was allowed and practised on the up-grades, but only in this first race. This first T.T. was won by C. R. Collier on a Matchless at 38 1/2 miles an hour, the full course being 155 miles in length.

When the petrol allowance was abolished in 1909, the average speed rose to 49 miles per hour. On this occasion twin-cylinder engines of 750 c.c. were allowed to compete against singles of 500 c.c. This difference proved to be too great, and the size of the twins was reduced to 680 c.c. in 1910, 585 c.c. in 1911, and then to 500 c.c., since when all types have competed on equal terms. In 1911 the Junior T.T. race was started, the engine sizes being 300 c.c. for singles and 340 c.c. for twins, and the first Junior T.T. was won by P. J. Evans on a twin-cylinder Humber. Since then other T.T. races have been started for light-weights with a 250 c.c. capacity, ultra-lightweight (175 c.c.), and side-car outfits (600 c.c.), the first winners being R. O. Clark (Levis), J. A. Porter (New Gerrard), and F. W. Dixon (Douglas), respectively.

In 1911 the mountain course was used for the first time. This is approximately thirty-seven and a half miles in length. The start and finish is close to Douglas, and the route passes through Ballacraine, Kirkmichael, Ramsay, and over Snae Fell, and a very sporting course it is. Since this course has been in use the Senior T.T. winners have been as follows:

1911	O. C. Godfrey	Indian	47.5 mph
1912	F. A. Applebee	Scott	48.6 mph
1913	H. O. Wood	Scott	48.2 mph
1914	C. G. Pullin	Rudge	49.4 mph
1920	T. C. de la Hay	Sunbeam	51.7 mph
1921	H. R. Davies	A. J. S. (349 c.c.)	54.49 mph
1922	A. Bennett	Sunbeam	58.31 mph
1923	T. M. Sheard	Douglas	55.55 mph

The results for 1924 may be given in greater detail. The Senior T.T., over six circuits of the mountain course (226 miles, 760 yards), resulted as follows:

1.	A. Bennett	4.90 h.p. Norton	61.64 mph
2.	H. Longman	4.96 h.p. Scott	61.23 mph
3.	F. W. Dixon	4.94 h.p. Douglas	60.17 mph

FASTEST LAP:

F. W. Dixon	63.75 mph

THE JUNIOR T.T. (SAME DISTANCE) (350 C.C.):

1.	K. Twemlow	3.44 h.p. New Imperial	55.828 mph
2.	S. Ollerhead	3.44 h.p. Dot—J.A.P.	54.908 mph
3.	J. H. R. Scott	3.49 h.p. A.J.S.	54.55 mph

FASTEST LAP, RECORD IN THE RACE FOR ANY MACHINE:

J. H. Simpson	3.49 h.p. A.J.S.	64.54 mph

THE SIDE-CAR T.T. (FOUR CIRCUITS) (600 C.C.):

1.	C. H. Tucker	5.88 h.p. Norton	51.31 mph
2.	H. Reed	3.44 h.p. Dot—J.A.P.	43.8 mph
3.	A. Tinkler	3.48 h.p.—Matador Blackburne	42.49 mph

FASTEST LAP:

F. W. Dixon	5.96 h.p. Douglas	53.24 mph

LIGHT-WEIGHT T.T. (SIX CIRCUITS) (250 C.C.):

1.	E. Twemlow	2.46 h.p. New Imperial	55.44 mph
2.	H. F. Brockbank	2.49 h.p. Cotton	52.85 mph
3.	J. Cook	2.49 h.p.—Dot—J.A.P.	52.54 mph

FASTEST LAP:

E. Twemlow	58.28 mph

ULTRA-LIGHT-WEIGHT T.T. (THREE CIRCUITS), (175 C.C.)—FASTEST LAP:

J. A. Porter	52.618 mph

The Grand Prix races are run off very much on the same lines as the T.T., and in 1924 Bennett was equally successful in them. The continental courses are shorter than the Isle of Man course, and having no mountain climb they are also faster.

Hill-climbs take place all over the country at frequent intervals. The competitors are generally started singly and timed. This sometimes makes the proceedings rather lengthy when the entry is a large one, and the classes numerous. Permission has to be obtained for these events from the police authorities.

Speed trials are generally held on some private road where the speed limit does not apply, or on the sands.[1] There are several stretches in Ireland and Wales which are quite suitable, as well as a few in England, but sometimes the sands are damp and then the speeds are not high. Occasionally these speed trials are organized by the authorities of some seaside resort and take place on the parade, when kilometre or half-mile trials can be run off and high speeds attained.

Brooklands Track is the scene of most of the motor cycle racing in England. Here there is plenty of room for a large number of riders to start at the same time, and races are frequent all through the season. These are often of three or five laps; but frequently much longer and therefore much more interesting and important races are held and wonderful speeds are attained. Here the hour records are made, sometimes in races, sometimes in individual attempts. Interest is often added by handicapping,

1   In consequence of the difficulty of providing for the safety of the spectators, who insist upon strolling on the roads, thereby endangering themselves and the riders, and two accidents which occurred at Kop Hill, the Royal Automobile Club and the Auto-Cycle Union placed a ban upon speed contests in any place to which the public have access. This occurred a little before Easter 1925, and it stops all hill-climbs and speed tests on public roads until some method of ensuring the safety of those concerned is devised.

and occasionally very close finishes are witnessed. Great Britain has always been to the fore with singlecylinder motor cycles, but at one time America held the lead in racing with big twin-cylinder machines, and a large number of races have been won by the Indian and Harley-Davidson. This lee-way has now been made up, and the big British sports models can hold their own with any machines in the world, as a glance at the records at the end of this book will show very plainly.

Motor cycle racing is not without its danger, and therein possibly lies some of its fascination for young Englishmen. There have been fatalities both in the T.T. races and at Brooklands. In fact it has been reported that a certain R.A.F. pilot, known for his daring over the enemies' lines, once said that motor cycle racing was much too dangerous for him. Also it was said that the late Rear-Admiral Sir Robert Arbuthnot took to motor cycle racing to satisfy himself that his nerves were in good order.

To lessen the danger a special racing helmet has been designed by the Auto-Cycle Union. This is certainly not becoming, but it protects the head effectually, and leather garments afford considerable protection to the body and limbs. Riding in a long race makes considerable demands upon the stamina as well as the courage of the rider. Great concentration is necessary, as well as coolness and rapid decision. Only those in the pink of condition should ride in a race like the T.T.

CHAPTER XIII

NOTABLE MOTOR CYCLES

To describe in detail every motor cycle on the market is neither possible nor desirable in this little book; but some brief particulars concerning outstanding and typical designs may well be included.

The Norton.—Undoubtedly the most successful machine in the competitions of 1924 was the Norton, a very fine example of single-cylinder design. The engine has a long stroke, unusually long for a motor cycle, in comparison with the bore. Two sizes of engine are manufactured, one having a bore and stroke of 79 × 100 mm., which gives a capacity of 490 c.c., and the other being 82 × 120 mm. (capacity 633 c.c.). The latter is known as the Big Four, and was designed for use with a side-car; the former is the engine that has brought most renown to the manufacturers.

This engine is made in two types, the older, or touring model, having side-valves and a one-piece cylinder, while the latest model—that most suitable for racing—has overhead valves. In many respects the two models closely resemble each other. The outside appearance is in each case very neat, and at once suggests that it is the conception of a designer who knows his job, for a smooth exterior is a very real advantage—a fact not always recognized. The cylinders are of fine cast-iron covered with deep graduated fins for cooling purposes, the crank-cases of chill cast aluminium, the valves of high tensile steel specially treated so that breakages are unknown, and the outsides have a special surface finish to make cleaning easy.

The overhead valve model has a detachable cylinder head.

The valves are operated by long push rods, which are provided with their own return springs, and rockers mounted on the cylinder head; these rockers work in double-row roller bearings, all the rollers being carried in a single cage and the two sets widely spaced. This method of constructing the overhead rocker gear makes for silence in a part which is often noisy. Means are of course provided for adjusting the tappet clearances. An aluminium alloy piston is used, fitted with two rings and a floating gudgeon pin. Engine lubrication is controlled by a mechanical pump, and oil is carried in a separate tank. A two-lever B. & B. carburetter is standard, and the magneto may be a C.A.V. or M.L.

Transmission is by chains, through a three-speed gear-box with close ratios (4 to 1 on top, 5.6 to 1 on middle, and 7.2 to 1 on bottom), and a shock absorber in the rear hub. A gear-box with the usual ratios can be fitted if desired, and would be more suitable if a side-car is to be attached; but for solo riding close ratios are best, especially for the fast work for which this machine is intended.

The Scott.—The Scott is a machine that is in many respects different from others. Short references have already been made to the engine and the frame, and it has been stated that both are right in principle, but there is much more that may be written. The crank-case of the Scott engine is divided into two halves and is, in fact, two crank-cases with the flywheel and sprockets between them. This enables crank-case compression to be used, which, if the crank-case were all in one, would be impossible, as with one piston rising as the other falls there would be no compression to use. As the explosions in a two-stroke engine occur with twice the usual rapidity for any given speed, the heat has very little time to be dispersed, and consequently the Scott is water-cooled, and is the only water-cooled motor cycle engine at present on the market.

The engine is made in several sizes, all of which have the bore equal to the stroke or in excess of it. The Super-Squirrel engine of 498 c.c. has a bore and stroke of 68.26 mm., and its companion engine has the same stroke and bore of 74.6 mm. Water-jackets are cast with the cylinders in the usual way, and in addition these two engines are fitted with aluminium water-cooled heads. Roller bearings are used throughout, all parts are in constant thrust, and there are fewer moving parts than in a singlecylinder four-stroke, and there is no valve noise. Mechanical lubrication is used which is entirely automatic and worked by the engine in connexion with an adjustable sight-feed control. An Amac two-lever carburetter is standard, and a B.T.H. magneto is placed in a sheltered position behind the tank.

The transmission is by Renold chains, heavy type, and the primary chain (or chains) being in the centre is well protected from dust and mud; the rear chain is provided with a cover. In the two-speed models there are two primary chains, one on each side of the fly-wheel, and a selective clutch worked by the heel and toe operates the gears. The three-speed gear-box is the constant mesh type, and is controlled by a hand lever.

The Scott engine has the power of pulling well at low speeds, hence it can be geared much higher than is usual in motor cycle practice, but at the same time it is quite capable of turning over very fast when required, and it runs with the pleasant hum of a four-cylinder car. Owing to the special frame and low centre of gravity it holds the road very well; in this it may be assisted by the front fork, the moving parts of which slide in sleeves so that the movement is constant relative to the steering head and the amount of 'trail' thus unaffected. This means that a line drawn through the steering centres will meet the ground always the same distance in front of the point of contact of the tyre.

A few additional details are as follows: the two cylinders with their water-jackets form a single casting. Internal expanding brakes are used on both wheels. The rear wheel of a three-speed model can be removed without disturbing the brake or chain wheel.

The Indian.—The Indian Super-Chief is one of the largest

motor cycles on the market. In fact it has a larger engine than many light cars, and is therefore well suited to draw a heavy and fully loaded side-car over hilly roads. The Indian, too, had the distinction of being one of the first sprung-frame machines; two quarter elliptic laminated springs were anchored below the saddle and extended rearward, the front forks were sprung on the same principle, and the machine was very comfortable. The present model is fitted with balloon tyres instead of a spring frame, and therefore the inequalities of the road are absorbed to a large extent before they have any effect upon the wheels.

A vee-twin engine with cylinders at 42° and having a bore and stroke of 82 × 112 mm. is fitted to this machine. This gives a cubic capacity of 1204 c.c., and a horse-power rating by the A.C.U. formula of 12.04 h.p. An automatic Indian Schebler carburetter is used, which has variable air and fuel adjustments, and consequently can be set to give ample power and flexibility. Engine lubrication is carried out by means of an automatic mechanical pump, with a hand pump for occasional use.

The gear-box is built in one unit with the engine, and the primary drive is by helical gearing running in oil. Timken roller bearings are provided on the clutch side; the clutch is of the multiple disc type, also running in oil. Three speeds are provided, the top gear being 4.85 to 1 for solo use and 5.36 to 1 when a side-car is fitted. The final drive is by a chain. Two brakes are fitted to the rear wheel, one expanding within a drum, the other contracting around it. The front fork spring is adjustable to the weight of the rider—a very useful feature when a side-car is sometimes used, and the rods from the spring to the hub are in tension.

As on the majority of American motor cycles, the controls are worked on the twist grip system. The clutch is operated by the left foot, and the brake pedal is on the right. Other Indian models are the Scout and the Prince; the former has a twin engine of 5.96 h.p. and the latter is a new model with a single-cylinder engine of small size, 3.48 h.p.

The Douglas.—To Douglas Motors belongs the credit of introducing the horizontally opposed twin-cylinder engine—or flat twin, to give it a more convenient name. This has been made in various sizes, but the most popular size to-day is practically the same as that first introduced, *viz.*, 348 c.c. (bore and stroke 60.8 × 60 mm.). This size has long been called 2 3/4 h.p., but by the new A.C.U. rating it becomes 3.48 h.p. This model is supplied with a belt-drive and two-speed gear, or a chain-drive and three speeds.

The magneto is placed on top of the crank-case, where it is easily accessible for the purpose of adjustment, and driven by a train of gears from the engine. The valves are made of specially forged 18 per cent, tungsten, and are practically unbreakable; the crankshaft is a solid steel stamping machined all over, complete with balance weights and carried on strong ball-bearings with a double row of balls on the driving side. The piston is of special crucible cast-iron of 18 tons tensile strength, with two narrow rings at the top. Semi-automatic lubrication is employed—that is, a spring-returned hand pump, and a sight-feed controlled by a needle-valve. The oil is first fed to the front cylinder, which would otherwise not get its proper share. It then passes to wells in the crank-case, into which the big-ends dip and throw the oil into the rear cylinder.

An overhead valve engine of the same size, approximately, but having a bore and stroke of 57 × 68 mm., is also made. This engine has pistons of a special alloy, and is fitted into a frame with a very low saddle position. The gear-box is above the rear cylinder instead of below it, and the engine is mounted much lower in the frame. This engine has detachable heads and rockers lubricated by wicks and operated by tubular push rods. The big-ends are not split, as in the other engine, but the connecting rods are threaded over the crank-shaft, after which double-row roller bearings are put into place and balance weights clamped into position. This method of threading the connecting rods over the crankshaft was introduced on the A.B.C.

For use with a side-car a larger engine (68 × 82 mm. bore and stroke, 596 c.c) is made. This engine has a detachable head and hemispherical combustion chamber; the overhead rocker gear is lubricated by a grease gun. One of these machines went through the Bristol to Land's End Trial on top gear in bad weather without giving any trouble.

Four-cylinder Engines.—Four-cylinder motor cycle engines have been made in several countries, but in spite of the merits of four-cylinders they have in most instances been dropped. When considering those at present on the market pride of place must be given to the F.N., for it has been longest in existence. The F.N. engine used to be quite small in size, but its dimensions have been increased from time to time, until now, in its twenty-first year, it has a bore and stroke of 52 × 88 mm. and a capacity of 748 c.c. It is rated by its makers as 8 h.p., and is a very fine sidecar machine; it can also be ridden solo.

Overhead inlet valves are used; these are placed in the centre of the cylinder head and operated by long push rods and overhead rockers working in roller bearings. The large exhaust valves are placed in pockets at the side of the cylinders, allowing large cooling spaces between the latter and the valve seating. Aluminium pistons are employed and a multiple disc-clutch placed in the fly-wheel. The crank-shaft is hardened and carried on ball-bearings; the big-ends, lined with phosphor-bronze, are 1 1/8 inches in diameter, and the crank-shaft is consequently very stiff.

A four-cylinder Bosch magneto is used, and on the fully equipped models a Bosch lighting dynamo is also fitted in line with the magneto. The lighting set includes head, tail and side-car lamps, and supplies current for a Klaxon horn. The standard carburetter is an Amac with special F.N. fittings.

The engine and gear-box are built up as a single unit, the gear-box shafts being placed across the frame and driven by a bevel from the gear-box to the back axle. A slow-running chain is now used in place of the shaft-drive that has been for so long a feature of the F.N. Adjustment is provided for the bevel gear, and the chain is adjusted in the usual manner by moving the rear wheel; but the adjustment of one part of the transmission does not in any way upset the other. Placing a reducing gear in the form of a bevel between the engine and gear-box enables the gears to be run slowly, but imposes upon them greater stresses than if they ran at engine speed. A cush-drive is incorporated in the rear chain-wheel, so that the drive is exceedingly smooth, and the comfort of the machine is increased by the use of balloon, or low-pressure, tyres.

The Henderson is, in the main, on very similar lines, but the engine is very much bigger, having a bore and stroke of 68 × 89 mm. and a capacity of 1301 c.c. The makers rate this engine at 11.5 h.p., but the A.C.U. rating is 13.01 h.p. Side valves are used, which are interchangeable, and the exhaust valves are made of Silcrome steel. Die-cast alloy pistons are standard, but cast-iron pistons can be supplied if preferred.

A pressure-feed lubrication system is employed, which leaves the rider nothing to do but to keep the sump supplied with oil. In the matter of electrical equipment and transmission the Henderson is practically identical with the F.N., but the magneto and dynamo are Splitdorf and a Wico battery is used.

Henderson frame-construction is somewhat unusual, but entirely satisfactory. The lower part is duplex, but there is no tube from the saddle to the countershaft. The front wheel is attached to trailing links, the other ends of which join a fork in tension, and the weight is carried on a helical spring contained in a cylinder; a rebound spring is also fitted, and the whole is very strong. Both wheels run on Timken taper roller bearings, and balloon tyres are standard fittings.

The Levis.—An excellent example of the two-stroke light-weight type is the Levis, and moreover it was the first of that type. During the last eleven years it has been very successful in competition. The Levis engine is now made in two sizes, the smaller having a capacity of 211 c.c., with a bore and stroke of 62 × 70 mm., and the larger 247 c.c. with the same stroke, but the bore increased to 67 mm. The engine uses crank-case compression and is of the three port type, namely, induction port, through which the gas enters the crank-case when the piston is at the top of its stroke; transfer port, through which the partially compressed gas passes from the crank-case to the cylinder when the piston is at the bottom of its stroke, and exhaust port. The Popular model is fitted with semi-automatic lubrication, single gear and belt-drive; the more expensive models have two or three speeds, belt and chain, or all chain-drive and mechanical pump lubrication.

The cylinder is of close-grained cast-iron machined to close limits, not only in the bore, but in the ports, and finally ground dead true; the gudgeon pin is tapered, but not a tight fit, and held in its place by spring rings. A one-piece crank-shaft is used to ensure correct and permanent alignment; this is balanced with bob-weights; chilled phosphor-bronze bearings are used throughout, and a split big-end, which can be taken up when wear occurs; the connecting rod is of 40-45 ton tensile steel.

The Levis machines are small and light, but they are good hill-climbers and are capable of high speed.

It is well when stopping a Levis, even for a short time, to turn off the oil and petrol, but especially the former, for excess of oil, or too rich a mixture, will cause difficult starting and four-stroking, which means that the engine misses alternate strokes. A new engine must, however, have plenty of oil while running.

The A.J.S.—The little A.J.S. has won the Junior T.T. (for machines under 350 c.c.) on several occasions, the Senior T.T. once, in spite of having to compete against larger machines, and it holds the record for the fastest T.T. lap made by any machine, its speed on that occasion being just over 64 1/2 miles per hour. It also won the Speed Championship of Europe in 1924 at the record average speed of 71 m.p.h., the fastest lap speed being 76 m.p.h. (also a record). Both these rides were done by J. H. Simpson.

This machine has an overhead valve engine, the valves being operated by push rods and rockers and a detachable cylinder head. A close ratio gear-box is fitted which provides gears of 5.52, 6.78, and 10.3 to 1. Internal expanding brakes are fitted to both wheels. A straight-through exhaust pipe or the usual silencer and tail pipe can be supplied to order. Lucas magneto and Binks carburetter are standard fittings; the forks are made by the A.J.S. under Druid patents, and are fitted with shock absorbers. The transmission is by Renold chains, 1/2 inch pitch, 5/16 inch wide, and a shock absorber is fitted to the engine shaft.

The engine has a bore and stroke of 74 × 81 mm., and a capacity of 349 c.c.; the piston is aluminium alloy, and a roller bearing is fitted to the big-end. Besides the overhead valve model, side-valve engines are also made in this size (3.49 h.p.), and the machine has done very well in trials with a side-car attached.

Sporting A.J.S., with Overhead Valves

The larger A.J.S., a 7.99 h.p. twin, has made a great name for itself as a side-car machine *de luxe*. It is suitable for fast touring anywhere. Lucas Magdyno electric lighting is fitted. Lubrication is by means of a semi-automatic hand pump (a mechanical pump can be fitted as an extra); the engine has a detachable head and side valves. The wheels are quickly detachable and interchangeable; a spare wheel can replace any of those in use.

The side-car is well upholstered and provided with a wind-screen and side-screens; a luggage-carrier is also fitted.

The Triumph.—No descriptions of motor cycles would be complete without the Triumph, a machine which has been a model to many other makers, so much so that it may be regarded to a great extent as an example of the finest standard practice, not differing much from others, for the reason given above.

The four-valve model, however, which is known also as the Ricardo-Triumph, or more familiarly as the 'Ricumph,' is quite on different lines. It is largely the design of Mr H. Ricardo, and has overhead valves, two inlet and two exhaust. The inlet valves are masked as described in Chapter III. The stroke is longer than the earlier Triumph, *viz.*, 97 mm., and the bore 80.9 mm. (499 c.c.). This machine is very popular for fast touring, and never seems to get unduly hot.

At the Olympia Show of 1924, a new low-priced model was introduced which caused considerable interest and excitement. This has a side-valve engine of 494 c.c.; it is chain driven and has Druid forks, as have most of the other models. The Baby Triumph, with its two-stroke engine of 249 c.c. and a 346 c.c. four-stroke are the two smaller models; and a side-car machine of 550 c.c., are the three departures from the usual Triumph size, which is in the 500 c.c. class. Nothing is ever adopted for the Triumph until it has had a very extended trial.

APPENDIX

MOTOR CYCLE RECORDS

THE following is a list of the records for one mile or more and one hour and upward as passed by the Federation of International Motor Cycle Clubs, to the end of the year 1924. One or two records included in the complete list have been omitted because they are not records, since better times or distances have been made in the classes for smaller machines. Flying-start records are marked (f.s.); when a record is not marked in this way it is to be understood that it was made from a standing start. A flying-start means that fifty yards or so are allowed in which to get up speed before the timing commences. World's records for short distances (one mile and under) consist of the mean speed for the distance ridden in both directions. Records are divided into two divisions: I, for motor bicycles ridden solo, and II, for motor bicycles with side-cars attached.

DIVISION I.
MOTOR BICYCLES

CLASS 2. FOR MOTOR BICYCLES NOT EXCEEDING 75 C.C.

Record	Date	Track	Holder	Machine and No. of Cylinders	c.c.	Time or Distance	Speed
						h. m. s.	m.p.h.
Mile (f.s.)	6/ 7/24	Arpajon (France)	Chéret	Rovin (1)	74·8	.. 1 23·05	43·35
Mile	"	"	"	"	"	.. 1 39·525	36·27

CLASS 3. FOR MOTOR BICYCLES NOT EXCEEDING 100 C.C.

						h.	m.	s.	m.p.h.
Mile (f.s.)	6/ 7/24	Arpajon	Beaudelaire	Griffon (1)	98·86	..	1	1·85	58·24
Mile	"	"	"	"	"	..	1	14·855	48·11

CLASS 6. FOR MOTOR BICYCLES NOT EXCEEDING 175 C.C.

Distance						h.	m.	s.	m.p.h.
Mile (f.s.)	29/ 5/24	Brooklands	W. D. Marchant	Ariel—Blackburne (1)	173	..	..	49·74	72·38
Mile	6/ 7/24	Arpajon	Janin	Monet Goyon (1)	"	..	1	10·75	50·88
5 Miles (f.s.)	24/ 9/24	Brooklands	W. D. Marchant	Excelsior (1)	"	..	4	13·46	71·01
10 Miles	"	"	"	"	"	..	8	37·21	69·60
50 "	19/ 8/24	"	C. W. Johnston	Cotton—Blackburne (1)	"	..	52	13·99	57·43
100 "	28/ 5/24	"	W. D. Marchant	Ariel—Blackburne (1)	"	1	55	58·9	51·73
Time						Miles	Yards		
1 Hour	19/ 8/24	"	C. W. Johnston	Cotton—Blackburne (1)	"	56	1256		56·71
2 Hours	28/ 5/24	"	W. D. Marchant	Ariel—Blackburne (1)	"	103	1088		51·72

CLASS A. FOR MOTOR BICYCLES NOT EXCEEDING 250 C.C.

Distance						h.	m.	s.	m.p.h.
Mile (f.s.)	6/ 7/24	Arpajon	H. le Vack	New Imperial (1)	245	..	..	40·39	89·24
Mile	9/11/23	Brooklands	W. D. Marchant	Rex-Acme—Blackburne (1)	248	..	..	55·64	64·70
5 Miles (f.s.)	24/ 4/24	"	"	Zenith—Blackburne (1)	"	..	3	37·27	85·20
10 "	"	"	"	"	"	..	7	13·58	83·03
50 "	26/ 8/24	"	H. le Vack	Le Vack—J.A.P. (1)	"	..	39	48·31	75·36
100 "	"	"	"	"	"	1	21	29·33	73·63
200 "	6/ 9/24	"	H. M. Walters	Zenith—J.A.P. (1)	247	2	58	44·68	67·14
300 "	6/ 9/22	"	{ W. D. Marchant & W. L. Handley }	O.K.—Blackburne (1)	248	5	16	28·54	56·87
400 "	"	"	"	"	"	7	3	27·41	56·67
500 "	2/ 7/21	"	B. Kershaw	New Imperial—J.A.P. (1)	249	9	59	5·0	50·07
Time						Miles	Yards		
1 Hour	26/ 8/24	"	H. le Vack	Le Vack—J.A.P. (1)	248	75	756		75·43
2 Hours	"	"	"	"	"	146	847		73·24
3 "	6/ 9/24	"	H. M. Walters	Zenith—J.A.P. (1)	247	201	735		67·14
4 "	6/ 9/22	"	{ W. D. Marchant & W. L. Handley }	O.K.—Blackburne (1)	248	228	167		57·02
5 "	"	"	"	"	"	283	1089		56·72
6 "	"	"	"	"	"	341	917		56·92
7 "	"	"	"	"	"	396	1496		56·60
8 "	2/ 7/21	"	B. Kershaw	New Imperial—J.A.P. (1)	249	406	370		50·77
9 "	"	"	"	"	"	454	1292		50·52
10 "	"	"	"	"	"	500	1384		50·07
11 "	19/ 7/22	"	Mrs R. N. Stewart	Trump—J.A.P. (1)	"	506	695		46·03
12 "	"	"	"	"	"	556	57		46·33

CLASS B. FOR MOTOR BICYCLES NOT EXCEEDING 350 C.C.

Record	Date	Track	Holder	Machine and No. of Cylinders	c.c.	Time or Distance			Speed
						h.	m.	s.	m.p.h.
Distance									
Mile (f.s.)	27/ 5/24	Brooklands	H. le Vack	New Imperial (1)	344	..	..	40·4	89·11
Mile	31/10/23	,,	G. Dance	Sunbeam (1)	348	..	..	46·14	78·02
5 Miles (f.s.)	26/ 5/24	,,	H. le Vack	New Imperial—J.A.P. (1)	344	..	3	17·69	91·05
10 Miles	,,	,,	,,	,,	,,	..	6	43·89	89·13
50 ,,	2/11/23	,,	,,	,,	346	..	35	16·14	85·09
100 ,,	24/ 9/24	,,	,,	,,	,,	1	12	7·11	83·19
200 ,,	18/ 5/23	,,	,,	,,	344	2	34	24·91	77·71
300 ,,	8/10/23	Monza, Italy	A. Sbaiz & E. Gnesa	Garrelli (2)	348	4	32	49	65·98
400 ,,	,,	,,	,,	,,	,,	6	2	27·6	66·21
500 ,,	,,	,,	,,	,,	,,	7	33	32·8	66·14
600 ,,	,,	,,	,,	,,	,,	9	3	16	66·26
700 ,,	,,	,,	,,	,,	,,	10	36	34·4	65·98
800 ,,	,,	,,	,,	,,	,,	12	4	55	66·21
Time							Miles	Yards	
1 Hour	24/ 9/24	Brooklands	H. le Vack	New Imperial—J.A.P. (1)	346		84	1104	84·62
2 Hours	,,	,,	,,	,,	,,		166	1245	83·35
3 ,,	6/ 9/24	,,	,,	,,	,,		223	61	74·34
4 ,,	8/10/23	Monza, Italy	A. Sbaiz & E. Gnesa	Garrelli (2)	348		264	103	66·01
5 ,,	,,	,,	,,	,,	,,		330	1058	66·12
6 ,,	,,	,,	,,	,,	,,		397	434	66·21
7 ,,	,,	,,	,,	,,	,,		464	357	66·31
8 ,,	,,	,,	,,	,,	,,		529	1086	66·20
9 ,,	,,	,,	,,	,,	,,		596	395	66·18
10 ,,	,,	,,	,,	,,	,,		658	303	65·82
11 ,,	,,	,,	,,	,,	,,		726	1323	66·07
12 ,,	,,	,,	,,	,,	,,		794	682	66·20

CLASS C. FOR MOTOR BICYCLES NOT EXCEEDING 500 C.C.

	Date	Track	Holder	Machine	c.c.	h.	m.	s.	m.p.h.
Distance									
Mile (f.s.)	4/11/24	Brooklands	V. Horsman	Triumph (1)	498	..	..	37·61	95·72
Mile	31/10/23	,,	G. Dance	Sunbeam (1)	492	..	..	46	78·26
5 Miles (f.s.)	2/ 8/24	,,	V. Horsman	Triumph (1)	498	..	3	13·92	92·82
10 Miles	20/10/23	,,	,,	,,	,,	..	6	42·68	89·40
50 ,,	6/11/24	,,	,,	,,	,,	..	34	5·88	87·98
100 ,,	12/10/24	Montlhéry	Richard	Peugeot (2)	494	1	7	43·8	88·36
200 ,,	19/11/24	Brooklands	A. Denly	Norton (1)	490	2	22	58·16	83·93
300 ,,	21/11/24	,,	C. T. Ashby and H. M. Walters	Montgomery (1)	488	3	45	36·44	79·78
400 ,,	22/11/24	,,	D. R. O'Donovan, A. Denly, and W. L. Gard	Norton (1)	490	5	27	28·25	73·29
500 ,,	,,	,,		,,	,,	6	56	36·04	72·01
Time							Miles	Yards	
1 Hour	12/10/24	Montlhéry	Richard	Peugeot (2)	494		88	794	88·44
2 Hours	19/11/24	Brooklands	A. Denly	Norton (1)	490		168	389	84·11
3 ,,	21/11/24	,,	C. T. Ashby and H. M. Walters	Montgomery (1)	488		241	1088	80·54
4 ,,	,,	,,		,,	,,		316	1421	79·70
5 ,,	22/11/24	,,	A. Denly, W. L. Gard, and D. R. O'Donovan	Norton (1)	490		364	1092	72·92
6 ,,	,,	,,		,,	,,		441	595	73·55
7 ,,	,,	,,		,,	,,		504	457	72·03

CLASS D. FOR MOTOR BICYCLES NOT EXCEEDING 750 C.C.

RECORD	DATE	TRACK	HOLDER	MACHINE AND No. OF CYLINDERS	C.C.	TIME OR DISTANCE			SPEED
Distance.						h.	m.	s.	m.p.h.
Mile (f.s.)	6/ 7/24	Arpajon	Penn	Peugeot (2)	745	..	..	35·04	102·74
Mile	17/11/24	Brooklands	V. Horsman	Triumph (1)	605	..	..	44·69	80·55
5 Miles (f.s.)	15/10/24	,,	,,	,,	599	..	3	4·93	97·33
10 ,,	,,	,,	,,	,,	,,	..	6	23·55	93·85
50 ,,	29/ 9/24	,,	,,	,,	,,	..	33	38·38	89·18
Time							Miles	Yards	
1 Hour	29/ 9/24	,,	,,	,,	,,		89	440	89·25

CLASS E. FOR MOTOR BICYCLES NOT EXCEEDING 1000 C.C.

	DATE	TRACK	HOLDER	MACHINE	C.C.				
Distance						h.	m.	s.	m.p.h.
Mile (f.s.)	6/ 7/24	Arpajon	H. le Vack	Brough-Superior (2)	867	..	..	30·27	118·93
Mile	9/11/23	Brooklands	,,	Zenith—J.A.P. (2)	998	..	..	43·76	82·27
5 Miles (f.s.)	7/ 6/24	,,	C. F. Temple	Montgomery-Anzani (2)	996	..	2	44·20	109·62
10 Miles	,,	,,	,,	,,	,,	..	5	44·60	104·47
50 ,,	21/11/22	,,	H. le Vack	Zenith—J.A.P. (2)	998	..	32	43·56	91·71
100 ,,	17/11/22	,,	,,	,,	,,	1	6	43·40	89·29
200 ,,	6/ 9/24	,,	T. R. Allchin	,,	,,	2	17	29·91	87·27
300 ,,	21/11/24	,,	C. T. Ashby and H. M. Walters	Montgomery (1)	488	3	45	36·44	79·78
400 ,,	4/10/22	,,	C. F. Temple and T. R. Allchin	Harley-Davidson (2)	989	5	10	41·22	77·24
500 ,,	25/11/22	,,	{ J. H. Mathers and R. E. Dicker	Rudge (2)	998	6	40	12·43	74·96
600 ,,	,,	,,	,,	,,	,,	8	25	7	71·27
Time							Miles	Yards	
1 Hour	17/11/22	,,	H. le Vack	Zenith—J.A.P. (2)	998		89	1591	89·90
2 Hours	6/ 9/24	,,	T. R. Allchin	,,	,,		178	22	89·06
3 ,,	21/11/24	,,	C. T. Ashby and H. M. Walters	Montgomery (1)	488		241	1088	80·54
4 ,,	,,	,,	,,	,,	,,		316	1421	79·20
5 ,,	4/10/22	,,	C. F. Temple and T. R. Allchin	Harley-Davidson (2)	989		385	1712	77·19
6 ,,	25/11/22	,,	J. H. Mathers and R. E. Dicker	Rudge (2)	998		450	654	75·06
7 ,,	,,	,,	,,	,,	,,		519	1118	74·23
8 ,,	,,	,,	,,	,,	,,		570	615	71·29
9 ,,	,,	,,	,,	,,	,,		603	568	67·03
24 ,,	5-6/ 5/09	,,	H. A. Collier	Matchless (2)	862		775	1340	32·32

108

DIVISION II.
MOTOR BICYCLES WITH SIDE-CARS

CLASS B/S FOR SIDE-CAR OUTFITS NOT EXCEEDING 350 C.C.

RECORD	DATE	TRACK	HOLDER	MACHINE AND o. OF CYLINDERS	C.C.	TIME OR DISTANCE	SPEED
Distance						h. m. s.	m.p.h.
Mile (f.s.)	6/ 7/24	Arpajon	R. N. Judd	Douglas (2)	346	.. .. 49·265	73·07
Mile	25/ 3/24	Brooklands	C. E. Tottey	New Imperial—J.A.P. (1)	344	.. .. 64·91	33·46
5 Miles (f.s.)	24/ 7/23	,,	W. D. Marchant	Chater-Lea—Blackburne (1)	348	.. 4 16·20	70·25
10 Miles	,,	,,	,,	,,	,,	.. 8 45·52	68·50
50 ,,	8/ 8/23	,,	,,	,,	,,	.. 44 55·63	66·77
100 ,,	23/ 8/24	,,	,,	,,	,,	1 35 48·31	62·63
200 ,,	,,	,,	,,	,,	,,	3 14 29	61·70
300 ,,	5/11/24	,,	S. M. Greening an E. S. P estwich	Enfield—J.A.P. (1)	344	5 12 45·68	57·55
400 ,,	,,	,,	,,	,,	,,	7 2 44·48	56·77
500 ,,	1/ 8/22	,,	C. G. Pullin and J. D. Marvin	Douglas (2)	346	11. 44 4·04	42·57
Time						Miles Yards	
1 Hour	8/ 8/23	,,	W. D. Marchant	Chater-Lea—Blackburne (1)	348	67 384	67·22
2 Hours	23/ 8/24	,,	,,	,,	,,	123 1601	61·95
3 ,,	,,	,,	,,	,,	,,	184 1114	61·54
4 ,,	5/11/24	,,	S. M. Greening and E. S. Prestwich	Enfield—J.A.P. (1)	344	227 150	56·71
5 ,,	,,	,,	,,	,,	,,	287 637	57·47
6 ,,	,,	,,	,,	,,	,,	337 1245	56·28
7 ,,	,,	,,	,,	,,	,,	397 560	56·76
8 ,,	,,	,,	,,	,,	,,	452 25	56·50
9 ,,	,,	,,	,,	,,	,,	452 25	50·22
10 ,,	,,	,,	,,	,,	,,	452 25	45·20
11 ,,	31/ 8/22	,,	C. G. Pullin and J. D. Marvin	Douglas (2)	346	467 1721	42·54
12 ,,	,,	,,	,,	,,	,,	510 1623	42·57

CLASS F. FOR SIDE-CAR OUTFITS NOT EXCEEDING 600 C.C.

RECORD	DATE	TRACK	HOLDER	MACHINE AND o. OF CYLINDERS	C.C.	TIME OR DISTANCE	SPEED
Distance						h. m. s.	m.p.h.
Mile (f.s.)	26/10/24	Brooklands	V. Horsman	Triumph (1)	599	.. .. 43·62	84·53
Mile	14/11/24	,,	V. Anstice	Douglas (2)	596	.. .. 54·25	66·36
5 Miles (f.s.)	8/ 9/24	,,	V. Horsman	Triumph (1)	599	.. 3 48·66	78·72
10 Miles	,,	,,	,,	,,	,,	.. 7 50·32	76·54
50 ,,	12/ 7/24	,,	,,	,,	,,	.. 38 59·20	76·95
100 ,,	8/11/24	,,	,,	,,	,,	1 28 9·04	68·06
200 ,,	23/ 8/24	,,	G. H. Tucker	Norton (1)	588	3 2 36·44	65·71
500 ,,	23/ 9/22	,,	H. H. Beach	,,	,,	9 31 48·37	52·46
600 ,,	,,	,,	,,	,,	,,	11 23 38·86	52·65
Time						Miles Yards	
1 Hour	7/11/23	,,	V. Horsman	Triumph (1)	599	69 31	69·01
2 Hours	8/11/24	,,	,,	,,	,,	133 1419	66·90
3 ,,	26/ 8/24	,,	G. H. Tucker	Norton (1)	588	197 237	65·71
9 ,,	23/ 9/22	,,	H. H. Beach	,,	,,	473 1119	52·62
10 ,,	,,	,,	,,	,,	,,	525 381	52·52
11 ,,	,,	,,	,,	,,	,,	576 257	52·35
12 ,,	,,	,,	,,	,,	,,	631 1396	52·65

CLASS G. FOR SIDE-CAR OUTFITS NOT EXCEEDING 1000 C.C.

Record	Date	Track	Holder	Machine and No. of Cylinders	c.c.	Time or Distance		Speed
Distance						h.	m. s.	h.m.p.
Mile (f.s.)	6/ 7/24	Arpajon	H. le Vack	Brough-Superior (2)	867	..	.. 36·09	99·74
Mile	20/10/24	Brooklands	J. P. Riddoch	Zenith—Blackburne (2)	999	..	.. 48·30	74·52
5 Miles (f.s.)	31/10/23	„	H. le Vack	Zenith—J.A.P. (2)	996	..	3 23·90	88·27
10 Miles	„	„	„	„	„	..	6 59·91	86·14
50 „	25/8/23	„	„	Brough-Superior (2)	„	..	37 47·68	79·37
100 „	„	„	„	„	„	1	17 5·64	77·82
200 „	„	„	„	„	„	2	39 18·60	75·32
300 „	23/10/24	„	H. R. Harte and S. T. Glanfield	Coventry-Eagle (2)	„	4	28 37·21	67·00
400 „	„	„	„	„	„	6	1 10·79	66·45
500 „	„	„	„	„	„	7	35 54·08	65·80
600 „	„	„·	„	„	„	9	8 38·15	65·61
Time						Miles	Yards	
1 Hour	25/ 8/23	„	H. le Vack	Brough-Superior (2)	996	77	1303	77·73
2 Hours	„	„	„	„	„	151	1515	75·93
3 „	23/ 8/24	„	R. E. Humphreys	Harley-Davidson (2)	989	204	1318	68·25
4 „	23/10/24	„	H. R. Harte and S. T. Glanfield	Coventry-Eagle (2)	996	267	1183	66·92
5 „	„	„	„	„	„	330	1457	66·16
6 „	„	„	„	„	„	398	1187	66·44
7 „	„	„	„	„	„	462	1068	66·09
8 „	„	„	„	„	„	524	1482	65·60
9 „	„	„	„	„	„	590	1707	65·66
10 „	„	„	„	„	„	603	315	60·31
11 „	„	„	„	„	„	603	315	54·63

Since the above list was compiled the following new records have been made: Class B/S, at Brooklands, H. le Vack, on a Coventry-Eagle with side-car, rode the mile (flying start) at a speed of 79.95 m.p.h.; 5 miles (flying start), 76.184 m.p.h.; and 10 miles, 72.995 m.p.h. Class F, at Brooklands, F.R.M. Spring, on a Norton with side-car, rode for four hours at a speed of 58.76 m.p.h.; 5 hours, 58.22 m.p.h.; 6hours, 58.73 m.p.h.; 7hours, 56.98 m.p.h.; 8 hours, 56.57 m.p.h.; 9 hours, 55.95 m.p.h.; 300 miles, 58.27 m.p.h.; 400 miles, 57 m.p.h.; 500 miles, 56.67 m.p.h.

Class B/S, at Montlhéry, Col. and Mrs R. N. Stewart, rode a Rudge-Whitworth with side-car for twenty-four hours at a speed of 54 m.p.h., total distance 1300 miles.

The fastest speed ever officially credited to a motor cycle is 122.44 miles per hour. This speed was attained by H. le Vack, on a Brough-Superior at Arpajon in France. On the same occasion and on the same machine he also made the highest speed reached by a side-car outfit, 103.04 m.p.h. Both these records were made in the flying kilometre.

Printed in November 2023
by Rotomail Italia S.p.A., Vignate (MI) - Italy